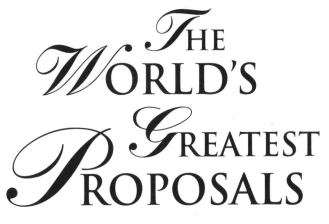

The World's Greatest Proposals

75 STORIES OF LOVE, CREATIVITY AND SPONTANEITY

BY FRED CUELLAR

CASABLANCA PRESS®
A DIVISION OF SOURCEBOOKS, INC.®
NAPERVILLE, ILLINOIS

Published by Sourcebooks, Inc.
P.O. Box 4410, Naperville, Illinois 60567-4410
(630) 961-3900
FAX: (630) 961-2168

Library of Congress Cataloging-in-Publication Data

Cuellar, Fred.
    The world's greatest proposals: 75 stories of love, creativity and
    spontaneity/ Fred Cuellar.
      p. cm.
    ISBN 1-57071-579-3 (alk. paper)
      1. Marriage proposals. I. Title

GT2650 .C83 2000
392.4—dc21

                                            00-041981

        Printed and bound in the United States of America
            DR 10 9 8 7 6 5 4 3 2 1

Table of Contents

Preface

In the summer of 1991, I sat down to write a book about diamonds. How to examine one, grade one, appreciate one, and above all how to buy one. When I was done I titled my new book simply *How to Buy a Diamond*. The book was chugging along when a publishing house named Sourcebooks added it to their list in 1996. The book took off!

Practically overnight *How to Buy a Diamond* became the No. 1 book on diamonds and it remains there to this day. Even if you find yourself in China browsing the bookstores you'll probably find a copy in Chinese on the shelves.

This book is, to a certain extent, a by-product of the first one. In my book on diamonds I included a chapter called "Will you marry me?"—a kind of how-to guide for guys on developing their own unique and special proposals. I also added a half-dozen or so of some of my favorite proposal stories. Little did I know that reading one good proposal story is like trying to eat just one potato chip…it's impossible. Thousands of requests came in for more proposal stories.

I reached out to all my readers through magazines, media, and my website at www.thediamondguy.com and asked them to tell me their proposal stories. The proposals came flooding in. Some will make you laugh. Some will make you cry. Some will even make you shake your head and wonder why. Of course it would be impossible to print all the wonderful stories we received, so we only chose the best of the best. With the wonderful help of my darling wife, loving family, and a staff of great assistants led by Lesa Smith and Blanca Cortez, we poured over thousands of proposals to bring you what you now hold. It is our hope that the proposal stories bring you as much joy as they did the participants themselves. —*Fred Cuellar*

P.S. As a bonus, I have added the original chapter "Will you marry me?" from *How to Buy a Diamond* as a guide for all you future proposers.

My Ship Came In

I am a sailor in the Navy, and I met my fiancée at a bar in Hong Kong. Little did I know that this was to be the woman of my dreams—as you can imagine, I was simply thinking about having a good time in port. (The rumors sometimes have merit.)

We spent a wonderful two days together and had a whirlwind romance until I departed. I continued to keep in touch with her via email and the phone. Upon my return to homeport, I arranged to have her meet me for a vacation to Bali, followed by Borneo. It was a fantastic vacation and I knew she was "the one" when we watched the sunrise atop Mt. Kinnabalu in Borneo. However, I kept my intentions guarded.

Later that month, I got called to take part in Operation Southern Watch. I left port and headed for the Persian Gulf. While out at sea, I thought about the woman I loved and daydreamed about all the neat places we still needed to go and enjoy together.

While in the Persian Gulf, I found myself in Dubai for an extended period of time. We decided that she should come out to visit me. We had talked before about her coming to visit me, but now the opportunity had made itself available. I had been contemplating marrying her, but I hadn't decided how to pop the question. Needing a plan, I decided to start with the experts at the Ritz Carlton in Dubai. They carefully guided me through the planning stages and offered tasteful suggestions at every turn. With the groundwork now laid, I simply needed to execute the plan without catastrophe. That would be the trick, since I was very nervous.

My fiancée arrived from London extremely jet lagged, so we headed directly to the hotel from the airport. The concierge greeted us at the door and whisked us straight away to our room. Once settled, my fiancée caught up on her sleep, got a manicure and a massage, and went for a dip in the pool. I busied myself with putting the finishing touches on the evening. The concierge recommended a quaint little Lebanese restaurant in downtown Dubai followed by a nightcap at the hotel bar. He also mentioned having a few surprises planned for our return, but offered no details.

I gave my fiancée a set of pearl earrings and a pearl pendant necklace right before dinner to set the mood for the evening. She was happy, but not as thrilled as I had envisioned she might be.

Dinner was delicious as we watched the belly dancers and feasted. My fiancée wanted to stay and watch the dancers, but I was feeling a bit anxious about the rest of the evening's events. In the taxi, my fiancée commented on how quiet I was during dinner (which is strange for me) and accused me of being "up to no good." When we returned to the hotel, the entire staff was watching us with big smiles as we headed toward the bar. This did not go unnoticed by my fiancée. She commented on how "attentive" the staff at the hotel was and once again voiced her suspicion that I was up to something.

We had a hurried nightcap (thanks to me) and started toward our room. A hotel manager joined us as an escort. We passed by our original suite and headed to another wing of the hotel.

Unbeknownst to me, the hotel had arranged for us to have the honeymoon suite for the evening and it was simply overwhelming. In the room was a dozen red roses, a bottle of champagne, a half-dozen strawberries (decorated in little chocolate tuxedos), a hot bath with flower petals and oils in it, two Cohiba cigars, a snifter of Remy Martin Cognac, and candles lit around the entire suite for ambiance. I was awestruck! The hotel staff had moved all of our luggage to this room and had placed our belongings identically to how they had been in the first room. My fiancée, still thrown off from the pearls, hadn't quite figured out what was going on and simply thought this was my big surprise for the evening.

She got ready for the bath and I poured the champagne. I slipped her ring into her glass and took it to her in the bedroom. I proposed a toast to "our love" and nervously raised my glass to my lips. My hands shook as she took her first sip of champagne. She didn't even notice the ring in the glass! She did, however, notice my shaking hand and commented on how I was still acting strange. I quickly ran through my mental Rolodex of toasts and came up with another beauty. (I was so nervous that I honestly can't remember what I toasted to! Maybe "to the Navy"?) With this sip, she noticed the ring and let out a gasp of surprise. She quickly gulped down the remainder of the champagne and plucked out the ring. I took the ring from her, got down on one knee, and asked her to marry me as she sat on the edge of the bed. She said yes with tears in her eyes. I let out a huge sigh of relief and there was much rejoicing until we were interrupted by a knock. At the door I found a bellboy burdened with a huge tray of passion fruit, appropriately enough.We stayed up until 4 A.M. planning our future together.

I found out later that the pearls had completely thrown off my fiancée. She was hoping I would pop the question while she was visiting, but wasn't sure it was going to happen. When she got the pearls, she was convinced that we were not going to get engaged in Dubai and was a bit disappointed.

It was a truly wonderful experience I will never forget. I am fortunate to have met the woman of my dreams and plan on returning to the hotel for our fiftieth wedding anniversary.

The Little Red Box

My boyfriend, Larry, and I were getting ready to leave for a cruise to Mexico, but it was also my mother's birthday. So we decided to take my mother and father out for dinner before we left. As we approached the restaurant, Larry asked my family and I to go on in, saying that he would follow. Well, some time passed and he finally returned. We finished our dinner, and when the check arrived, the server automatically gave the bill and a little red box to me. Well, I was quite surprised and a little upset—one, it was not my birthday, it was my mother's day; and two, I never said that I was paying for the bill. I quickly passed the box to my mother, along with the gift from Larry and me, and gave the check to Larry.

As my mother was opening the box, Larry looked concerned while my mother began to smile and almost cry at the same moment. Meanwhile, my father and I were very curious!

"Well, what is it?" my father snapped.

My mother then gave the box to me and said, "This is for you! Happy Engagement!"

I just began to cry! The entire side of the restaurant where we were sitting began clapping while Larry asked my mother and father for my hand! —*Cassandra Daniel*

Drive-Thru Proposal

Well, he's quite the shy guy. He took me all over Vancouver, B.C., trying to find the perfect place to propose (of course, I didn't know that!). We started out going through Stanley Park and stopping for a walk. Then we got back in the car and drove to another scenic spot in the western end of Vancouver along the beach and took another long walk. I started to get hungry, so we decided to start on the forty-minute drive home. He stopped alongside the road in a grove of trees and I demanded to know why we were stopping where there was obviously no food. He simply replied, "I don't know," and pulled back out onto the road.

We pulled into the drive-thru of McDonald's and I turned and asked, "Why are you acting so strange? Do you have a ring in your pocket or something?"

As I spoke, I put my hand into his pocket and pulled back, startled. Sure enough, there was something in there and I was proposed to in the drive-thru at McDonald's! —*Marguerite Eyeford*

The Telltale Heart

My boyfriend and I had just finished dinner at a popular Mexican restaurant in Oklahoma City when I suggested we go for a nice walk to pass the time until our movie began at 10:30. We headed to Lake Hefner, one of our favorite spots, with me driving his new black Firebird for the first time.

We took off for our favorite spot, where we had our first kiss two and a half years earlier. As we walked, I commented on how the weather was almost identical to that night we first kissed; he agreed and we kept on. When we reached our destination, he embraced me and I kept close to keep warm because the wind was chilly. We held each other by the water; it was so beautiful.

After a few minutes of embracing I noticed that his heart was beating like crazy. I asked him about this and he responded that he was a little out of shape. I laughed and said not that out of shape. I then started worrying that something was wrong with him. Then he said, "Well, maybe this is the reason."

"What!?"

"Look!"

I looked up to a ring held high in the air. All I could do was look at it and say, "Oh, my gosh!"

He said, "Will you marry me?"

He then scared me to death because he grabbed me tight and gave me the biggest kiss in the world and started bawling. I have never seen him cry so hard. He was holding me and sobbing. One tear trickled down my cheek, but then I got ecstatic. I said, "Oh Tim, I love it, I love you!"

He then got down on his knee (how I have always requested) and asked the question once more. He knew the answer, but I said yes emphatically anyway. For about ten minutes he sobbed and all I could do was giggle and squeeze him and tell him how happy I was. After he had gained his composure somewhat I said, "Please, put it on my finger!"

He did and we then headed to my house, where I still live with my parents, to share the happy news. He drove home because I was too excited. The entire ride home I had the lights on just admiring my new ring.

I was totally surprised, although I had been waiting since Christmas for this day. He had asked my father in December for my hand, but was having a "scared feeling," so he put it off. Weeks earlier I had decided that there was no hurry and I wasn't going to guess when it would be anymore. It was a perfect surprise! He told me later that night that it was so funny that I had mentioned going for a walk because it was exactly what he was going to ask me to do because he

8

wanted it to be special. He knew that I would have guessed if it were something elaborate. He had it all planned out, even knowing a fake movie and time. He said I sure made his job easier by mentioning it first. It was incredible! —*Emily Logan*

The Golden Egg

I was expecting a ring on my birthday at the end of April. I thought we would go out for a nice dinner or something similar, but my boyfriend (now fiancé) had something else in mind.

The day before Easter, Ken and I had a party honoring friends of ours who were about to have baby. Ken does not keep secrets very well, so he told everybody at the party, excluding me, about his plans to propose. He even showed everybody the ring, which was in the office, and the detailed plan of how he was going to propose. When I asked him why he was taking people in and out of the office, he said he was showing them our new cable modem. I thought this was a bit odd, but I naively believed him. Luckily for him, I did not find out about his plans until the next morning.

On Easter morning, I slept in until about 10 A.M. Ken is an early riser, so he awoke about 6 A.M. He woke me up frequently between 6 and 10 A.M. to ask me how much longer I was going to sleep. Little did I know that he had plans and was chomping at the bit (since it is so hard for him to keep a secret). Around 10 A.M., I woke up and took a shower. I then sat down on the couch in my pajamas with a towel wrapped around my head. I guess Ken could not wait a moment longer. He brought out an Easter basket and said, "Happy Easter!"

I was surprised because we had not exchanged Easter baskets previously. The basket was filled with candy and plastic eggs with notes inside them. The notes said things like, "This is good for one whole house cleaning (with one week's notice)." "This is good for five back rubs." "This is good for five unreasonable, slave-like favors in the middle of the night," etc.

Finally, I had read all the notes and of course was very delighted with my surprise Easter basket, but Ken said, "I think you may have missed one."

There was one golden egg left. Inside the egg was a lovely diamond ring with a note: "I love you and want to spend the rest of my life with you. Will you marry me?" Ken then got down on one knee and asked me in a shaking voice and with a shaky hand to marry him. I, of course, accepted. —*Teresa McWhirt*

Pieces to the Puzzle of My Heart

It all began the day before Valentine's Day as we began our trip to Michigan for a weekend getaway. I was given a homemade card of two large red hearts fastened together at the top. On the front was written "Happy V-Day '98." On the inside was a sweet message that said, "Happy Valentine's Day, with all the love in my heart." On the other side of the card a jigsaw puzzle was drawn. He then told me that I would have to find each of the pieces to the puzzle to receive my gift.

About an hour later, he asked me to get his sunglasses out the glove compartment. When I opened it up I found the first piece to the puzzle. On one side the letter *E* cut out from a magazine was pasted, and the other side had the word *close*. I asked if I was supposed to know what this meant, but he said that I would find out eventually. When we arrived at the little cottage we did a little unpacking, then relaxed in front of the TV. When it was time for bed, I went to the bathroom to get myself ready. In my cosmetic bag I found a second piece. This one had a tin man pasted to one side, and the word *to* on the other. This piece fit (tin man side up) to the left of the *E*. I became very curious about what the rest of the pieces would tell me.

The next morning, after a romantic night together, I found a few more pieces in my suitcase and around the cottage, each leading me to the solution. Later, he asked me if I had found all the pieces. I said all but one. He then had me put those pieces together. On one side, "Will You Be My Valentine" was spelled out in the following way: first a picture of Will Smith, then the letter *U*, next a picture of a bumble bee, followed by the letter *M* and an eye, next came a picture of Tiffany Amber-Thiessan (as Val on *90210*), then the letter *N*, next came the tin man, and last was the letter *E*. The last piece was the only one missing. When I flipped the pieces over and put them in the same order it said, "Your present is close to my heart."

I found the last piece in the breast pocket of his coat. It had a little girl dressed in a wedding gown, followed by a question mark. Attached to the piece was a string, and at the end of that was the most beautiful ring I had ever seen. He then dropped to one knee, quickly untied the string, slipped the ring on my finger, and popped the famous question, "Will you marry me?" I quickly answered yes as I bawled. This was the happiest moment of my life. —*Kristina Perrault & Ken Holmes*

Message in the Grass

We had just moved in together six months prior and were completing a remodeling project. Over this time, I had kind of given up on the marriage thing for awhile, due to all of our savings going into the house. Anyway, one night I had to run into town to do some errands. I had asked Rich to please get the weeds pulled from the garden while it was still light out.

I returned home around 8 P.M. and ran into the house to get dinner going. Rich came in and mentioned how nice the field of oats were doing in the back field, and wanted me to look out the window, but I was too busy at the time. We finished dinner and cleaned up, then Rich insisted that we go out and look at the nice job he had done on the garden. Well, I got out there and found he hadn't done a damn thing! So I started to do my womanly thing, complain, when all of a sudden I looked up and noticed that he had done something— he had mown "Will you marry me?" into the lawn! We have an acre of lawn that sits on a slight hill, so it was totally legible. He then got on his knees and repeated the question with our golden retriever by his side.

The ring was unbelievable and so is he! Of course, I said yes. The next day we went to the top of one of the silos and took some really nice pictures. All in all, I have to say he made that day one to remember. I'll always have this dreamy tale to tell. What can I say—he's a keeper! —*Heidi Hendrickson & Richard Rashke*

He Shoots, He Scores!

My boyfriend, our parents, and I attended an Austin Ice Bats hockey game on the day after Valentine's Day. As we entered the arena and took our seats, Tom's seat number was called for the chance to shoot a hockey puck to win a picnic table. During the first intermission, we went down to the ice—I was going to take photos of Tom making his "winning" shot. I had no idea it was all a setup—Tom did make the shot and won the table; then he asked the announcer for the microphone and got down on one knee in front of an arena full of people and asked me to marry him. It was a total surprise, and very romantic!
—*Leticia Youngblood & Thomas Dougherty*

Letters in the Sand

John planned a trip to Mystic, Connecticut, where we stayed at a bed and breakfast on the beach. We spent the day sight-seeing and lounging on the beach. Later, I went for a walk along the beach, but John stayed behind to "catch up on his reading." I came back a little later. John met me along the way and wanted to go back to the bed and breakfast to get ready for dinner.

A little later, we set out for a cute little restaurant up the road. On the way, John insisted that I go with him to see something on the beach. At first I didn't want to go and asked what it was. I was fussy the whole time, but that's how I am—I don't do well with surprises.

Well, to finish our story, while I was gone, John had written out in the sand with seashells: "Marry me, Dana." He showed me his handiwork, then handed me a small blue box and asked me what I was doing for the next sixty years or so. I started to cry and he hugged me and told me he loved me. I said yes. How could I not? I love him more than anything. We then called our families, took some pictures of his work of art, had a wonderful dinner, and sat up all night in front of the bed and breakfast, talking on the beach, and watched the sunrise. —*Dana Louise DeBiase & John Paul Barti*

The Serenade

Matthew has been my best friend for years. He is also an absolutely hopeless romantic, but I never thought he would propose the way he did.

Matthew and I were at the concert of a band he knew well and worked with once in a while. When it was almost over, he said he had to go to the bathroom. I was relieved when the band was called back for an encore, because this gave him a few more minutes before the crowd gathered. Next thing I knew, there were two guys onstage—Matthew at the piano and another guy, Craig, at the drums. They were both wearing the same outfits as when I first had seen them in concert a few years back. Matthew started to play and said into the microphone, "This next song is for the girl I met five years ago in my first performance, and the girl I hope is my last." He was talking about me!

The next thing he did was completely unexpected—at the the end of the song, he came down with the microphone, got on one knee, and sang me my proposal. I cried very hard and said yes! It was an awesome end—or should I say beginning—to an incredible night. —*Tonia Lynn Nadeau & Mathew J. Byers*

Jailhouse Rock

It was Saturday and I was supposed to pick up my girlfriend, Jami, at 3:00 P.M. to go to a carnival. Well, on my way, I stopped and called her on my cell phone to tell her that I had just been pulled over by the police and that I would be late. (My voice was very distraught and full of anger.) At 3:30 P.M. she received another call from me telling her that I had been arrested for insulting an officer and attempting to intimidate an officer. I told her that they were going to press charges and that she had to come down and bail me out of jail and bring a check for one hundred fifty dollars. An officer then came on the line to give her directions to the police station.

As I waited for my sweetie to come down and bail me out, they took me downstairs to a containment cell, where they positioned a camera so all of the ladies up in dispatch could watch me pop the question. They also turned on a speakerphone to catch all of the audio. (I had called nine to ten different police departments to help me hatch my proposal plan, and this one was the only one that would help me—I was very grateful.) When she showed up, the officers went through the paperwork with her and said it would be a few minutes before it was ready. The watch commander then asked her if she would like to see the "prisoner." She agreed with a horrible look on her face.

They took her downstairs to my containment cell, where she found me with my head buried in my hands. Her face was white as she came into the cell and sat down. I explained that they were going to press charges and that I thought that this was going to go on my record. Although she was upset with the situation, she offered her support and said that we would get through this. (Side note: this is why I love her!) I then handed her a note that I described as an arrest sheet and said that she should read it. The note went like this: "As long as you are here with me, they can lock me up and throw away the key—forever. Jami, will you marry me?"

She was very confused and it took a minute or so for everything to sink in. By then, I was on my knee with a beautiful ring shining towards her. Her first reaction led me to believe that she would leave me there to rot in jail, but when she finally realized what was really happening, she threw her arms around me and said, "Yes! Yes! Yes!" Then all of the ladies in dispatch yelled and cheered for us through the speakerphone. They had gotten the whole thing on camera and heard every word of my proposal. We then went and got our mug shots and I promised that she never would have to do this again…I hope! As it turned out, she had no idea of what was going to happen and was ready to contact her lawyer to help me. The plan went on without a hitch, thanks to my friends at the Leawood Police Department.

We finished off the weekend by going to a resort north of the city, where she was greeted by a dozen roses in the presidential suite and received a massage the next morning. We spent the whole weekend talking about my life of crime and enjoying every minute of it. Who says crime doesn't pay? —*Patrick Murphy*

Promises of Love

Don picked me up from the Columbus airport that afternoon. We had spent winter break apart and missed each other quite a bit. I had left sunny Florida that morning so we could spend New Year's Eve and the two-year anniversary of our first date together. We exchanged presents and he asked me if I wanted to go for a walk, something we do often. We went to a cute little park where we like to hang out. We played in the snow and came upon a little wooden bridge where he told me he wanted to give me my annivarsy present early. My heart jumped at the thought of an engagement. He quickly informed me that it wasn't a ring, so I chilled out.

He proceeded to give me my gift—a list of wonderful promises. He promised to love me unconditionally like God would have him do, and he promised me everything that he had, especially his heart. He ended it with "if you would be my wife!" I was so surprised! I accepted, of course.

He then reached into his pocket and pulled out a ring box. I said, "I thought it wasn't a ring!"

He replied, "Your present wasn't the ring, it was the promises!"

The ring was truly a sacrifice on his part. Being college students, we are both on a really tight budget. I could not have been more appreciative of his sacrifice for my beautiful ring, but since he is a man of his word, those promises are worth even more than gold and diamonds! —*Peggy Cisneros & Don Arnott*

On the Air

I've often accused my fiancé, David, of not being romantic enough. So I guess he felt that his proposal had to be special—and it was. He's a detective in the Bronx and on Christmas Eve he had to work, so he asked me to pick him up. I happened to have the day off from my job as a reporter, so I dressed in my worst pair of jeans and a T-shirt and went to get him. He gave me the sweetest kiss when he got in the car.

As we approached the door to our apartment, I could smell candle wax in the hallway and commented that one of our neighbors must be burning a lot of candles. When I opened the door, there were lit candles everywhere! All over the coffee table, on the dining room table, everywhere you looked. On one table there was a bottle of champagne on ice and two glasses. I thought, "Wow, what a Christmas present!" He asked me to pour the champagne while he turned on the radio. Right on cue I heard the anchors at my radio station say, "David has something special to say to the woman he loves." Then they played a tape with his voice proposing to me on the air!

When I turned to look at him, he was down on one knee with a beautiful two-carat diamond ring in his hand. As I was about to say yes with tears in my eyes, the anchors at my radio station piped up, "Darlene, call us back with your answer!"

What I didn't know was that my handsome guy who's kind of shy, had called the boss at the station and arranged to pre-record the proposal and have it played at exactly the right time. He also had my girlfriend set up the candles while I was picking him up from work. Both of our families were in on it and were listening at home. The phone didn't stop ringing and there were tears of happiness for days. —*Darlene Pomales & David Rodriguez*

Goin' to the Chapel

My fiancé's sister is married to a Lutheran minister in a nearby town. Their home is connected to the chapel, community center, and the church. I love the chapel there and tend to be drawn to it each time we go to visit. It is very small, brightly lit, and extremely spiritual. We had been playing with his sister's children and my fiancé's son in the community center when I asked if it would be OK to go to the chapel. We all started toward the chapel.

When we got to the chapel, my fiancé, Brian, pretended to be walking me down the aisle. He let go and went to the end of the aisle and stood where the prospective groom stands. I continued to joke about how on our wedding day, I was going to "ease on down the road," and danced the whole way down. I told him to kiss the bride, and then I began to walk away.

He said, "Hey!" I turned around and he was down on one knee. He said, "Well, will you marry me?"

Since we had been joking the whole time (and we joke around a lot!) I said, "Shut up! You are not even funny. Get up off of your knee!" I turned to walk away and he grabbed my hand.

He said, "I am serious. Will you marry me?"

I noticed that with his free hand he was trying to turn the ring around. When I saw the ring, I knew he was serious. Of course I said yes!

He had planned to propose to me all along in the chapel, it just so happened that I requested to go in there. It meant a lot to me that he noticed how much the chapel means to me and that he chose such a spiritual, romantic way to propose. To top it all off, he had asked my parents for permission to marry me the week before! —*Jayne Conner & Brian Runyon*

The Winning Ticket

The proposal took place at our annual scuba diving banquet. Arriving at the banquet, we purchased raffle tickets for the various prizes they were giving away throughout the night. Shortly after the raffle began, we started to win. First, we won dinner for two at a restaurant called In-and-Out. Next we won two tickets to a scuba show, along with a one-year subscription to *CA Diving News* and a Monterey dive magazine. Our next winning raffle ticket produced another one-year subscription to *CA Diving News*. The winning continued with another free dinner for two at a Mexican restaurant, followed by a free disposable camera and free processing. Next was a mystery gift, and once again I held the winning raffle ticket.

When I went up to get the prize, the MC was holding a small box, which he told me to open. I turned around and there was Larry. I saw that little box and Larry and I knew what was going on, but I was in shock. I opened the box as Larry said, "Elaine, I've known you twelve years of my life, will you be my wife?"

I was estatic and whispered a yes with a hug and kiss. The ring consisted of two beautiful dolphins head to tail in a circle with a diamond in the middle.

Upon sitting back down, the president of the club announced, "Larry, I've known you eight of those twelve years and it's about time."

But the winning did not stop there. We went on to win registration in karate classes, a two-night stay in Las Vegas, and a bottle of wine. I was definitely the luckiest person there that night! —*Elaine Samson & Larry Riendeau*

Floating on the Clouds

It was coming up on Valentine's Day and my boyfriend told me that he wanted to do something special that year, which in itself is not so unusual because he loves to go away for weekends and do special things. So he arranged a whole weekend for us while I visited my family in Germany.

When Valentine's Day arrived, we got in our car and he started driving, but I had no clue where we were actually going. After an hour's drive, I figured out the destination—Newport, Rhode Island. When we arrived at our beautiful inn, it was pouring rain outside and very stormy, but nonetheless my boyfriend asked if I wanted to see the view of the waves in the ocean from the cliff-walk. Because we both didn't mind the storm and we both loved the ocean with all its power, I agreed.

We fought our way through gusty winds in the direction of a spot we both knew would have the best view. When we arrived, we were totally wet and our umbrella was nearly destroyed, but we were happy because it was unbelievably beautiful. All of a sudden, my boyfriend went down to his one knee right into a pit of water, and I started wondering what he was doing down there fiddling at his jacket. He proposed and reminded me that this was the spot where I decided one year ago that I was going to leave my home country, Germany, to be with him. We had known each other for ten years—since we were sixteen—and kept each other dear over the distance.

When we got back to the inn, the room was decorated all over with flowers and candles, the whirlpool was set for a hot bath, music was playing, and the champagne was chilled. It was so amazing that I felt like I was floating on clouds! *—Daniela Hellmann & Daniel Kinsbourne*

The Surprise Party

I had always told my boyfriend (now fiancé) that I would want to celebrate immediately with all of our family and friends as soon as we got engaged! I knew that that we'd have plenty of time to be romantic and share memories alone in due time.

So, on my twenty-sixth birthday, he had arranged to have drinks at a very cool bar in Chicago and then go to the restaurant next door for dinner. When he came to pick me up for the evening, I noticed he was empty-handed and hadn't brought over my birthday gift (how could a girl not notice!). He told me that the gift was at his apartment because it wouldn't fit in his car (yeah, right). He said that we could stop to get the gift after dinner because we were going to meet up with friends later that night at one of our favorite bars.

Over drinks, he asked if I wanted to get my birthday gift then. I was very confused, because I thought the gift was golf clubs (since they would be too big to fit in his car). But I said yes and he looked me in the eye and asked me to marry him! I let out a scream and tears came streaming down my face as the whole restaurant cheered. We had a few more drinks and then ate dinner next door—but the best part was still to come!

We went to our favorite bar and I kept babbling about how we had to call our parents. When I walked into the bar, everyone yelled, "Surprise!" He had arranged a surprise party for me with both of our families and all of our friends. Only my father knew that it was actually a surprise engagement party and not a birthday party! My fiancé came through with flying colors because he actually had listened to me all along when I said I wanted to celebrate with all my family and friends! We had the time of our lives and I'll never forget it. —*Kelley O'Connell & Timothy Enright*

Frozen in Time

One night, while watching a program about Alaska, my fiancé, Scott, thought of the perfect place to propose to me—on a glacier! The only problem was, when he told me he wanted to go to Alaska for vacation, I objected. I wanted to go someplace warm like Mexico, the Carribbean, or Hawaii. After much persistance on his part, we ended up booking a cruise to Alaska.

Once the cruise was booked, we had to choose our shore excursions. He really wanted to take a helicopter tour to a glacier, where we would actually get out and explore the glacier! I didn't want to because I was afraid the helicopter would crash, but I finally agreed to it.

The first several nights on the cruise ship were wonderful. We were having the time of our lives when our ship stopped in Juneau, Alaska. There we boarded our helicopter to fly to the glacier. There were two helicopters going. I was so nervous (and later found out he was too, but for different reasons!). Once we landed on the glacier, we were free to roam around.

While I was exploring the glacier, Scott secretly told the pilot of our helicopter that he was going to propose to me, and to let him know when we were about to leave the glacier. After we had been on the glacier awhile,

Scott noticed the pilot walking around whispering to the others who were on the glacier with us—he knew the time had come! Then the pilot came up to me and said, "Hey, give me your camera and I'll take a picture of the two of you." I said OK and Scott and I found a nice place to pose for the picture.

Scott told me to look at the pilot, then said my name. When I looked over at him, he was on one knee, holding the ring. He said, "Will you marry me?"

I gasped, "Are you serious?" I was so surprised!

People started shouting, "Did she say yes? Did she say yes?" He said, "I don't know! Did you say yes?" And of course then I said yes! Everyone was clapping. One lady was crying and ran over to give me a huge hug! We got lots of congratulations. Scott had a beatiful speech planned, which he shared with me later, but he froze at that moment and couldn't say it!

The helicopter ride back was breathtaking. As we looked out over the beautiful glaciers, all I could think was how romantic it was of Scott to plan such an original, unforgettable proposal. I was so happy we went to Alaska instead of Hawaii! The whole trip was amazing!

While we were on the cruise, a little boy who was on the glacier with us came up to us to congratulate us. Then he asked, "Where are you gonna go on your honeymoon?" Hmmm…good question—how can we beat that trip? —*Renee Shvedowsky & Scott Johnson*

Under the Sea

My fiancé, Eric, is the most wonderful man in the world. Last September we planned a trip to Walt Disney World. My favorite park is Disney-MGM studios and my favorite Disney movie is *The Little Mermaid*. Eric and I could not wait until Friday because that was the day we were going to Disney-MGM. On Thursday, Eric insisted on having our picture taken with the characters at the Magic Kingdom. We met Mickey, Minnie, Ariel (the Little Mermaid), and about twenty more of our favorite characters.

On Friday, Eric and I slept in until 8:30 A.M. Disney-MGM opened at 8 A.M., so we jumped out of bed and began rushing around because in our minds we were late. When I was in the shower, Eric put the ring in his fanny pack. We arrived at 9:15 A.M. and went immediately to "The Voyage of the Little Mermaid"— our favorite attraction at MGM. We arrived just after the second show began. The usher at the door told us that the next show began at 10 A.M. Eric asked him if Joel was around and the usher said, "Are you Eric?" Eric said yes. As the usher called Joel, I asked Eric what was going on. He said that he arranged for us to meet Ariel after the show. (He works for the Disney Store in

Michigan so he arranged it before we left with the help of his supervisors.) I reminded him that we met her the day before at the Magic Kingdom. Eric said that she would be wearing a different pair of sea shells and he wanted another picture of us together. I just laughed. When Joel came out, Eric tried desperately to get rid of me, asking me questions like, "Do you have to go to the restroom? Do you want something to drink?" I knew at this point that something was up and I also knew that I was not going to go anywhere until I knew everything!

After the show, we met Ariel and Prince Eric in the lobby of the theater. Ariel asked us if we would like to see the things out of the treasure chest. Suddenly she pulled out a little white box and said, "Flounder brought this to me but I don't know what it is. Do you know, Eric?"

Eric said, "Gee, I don't know. Let's open it. Oh, it's a ring!" He turned it to me and said, "Colleen, will you become part of my world?" I just kissed him—I couldn't say anthing.

Prince Eric asked me, "Does that mean it is a yes?"

I then said, "Of course it is yes!" I turned to Ariel and said that now I had my own Prince Eric! Because of this proposal, we are having an "Under the Sea" theme at our wedding. —*Colleen Von Allmen & Eric LaCrosse*

Twenty-Four-Hour Celebration

I started planning my proposal to Amy right after we met, which means it took six months to plan. I wanted this day to be one that neither of us would ever forget! Both of us are only children, we were both spoiled as kids, and we both have vivid imaginations, so I had a tough task ahead of me. I did know that it had to be Arizona. A native of Phoenix, she talked of little else that cold winter in Ohio. How beautiful the desert was, how wonderful the long days of sun were, and on and on. My annual bonus from the office would provide the needed funds for the flight out and the special day. A friend of the family, who is a private jeweler, provided the needed stone: a nearly flawless ¾-carat princess cut diamond solitaire in a Tiffany mount. The baguettes would have to come later. While a personalized card from Hallmark surprised her with the tickets, I needed extra help to set the "trap." Long distance phone calls from the office to my "dream day team" in Arizona arranged the entire day down to the minute. This proposal was going to be a twenty-four-hour celebration!

We awoke bright and early in our Sedona hotel to a little white lie. I had to tell her we were going on a jeep safari, when what I had in mind was far more dramatic! Before the sun came up, we were dropped off in the middle of the desert amidst the roar of hot air blowers inflating three beautiful ballons. The ride was a first for us both. Watching the sun rise over the beautiful red mountains and mesas of Sedona at three thousand feet was nearly a religious experience. At thirty-five hundred feet, I couldn't wait any longer, so I asked everyone in the basket to scoot over because I had something I wanted to ask my girlfriend. "Oh, my God! Yes!" she shouted, and I carefully handed her the ring. (I would've jumped out after the rock if I had dropped it!) All was captured on our balloon mates' video camera. But the day was far from over!

After touchdown, the three balloons met for a champagne breakfast in the middle of the desert. After the news was passed around and many mimosa toasts were enjoyed, we headed back to our rental car for a trip up the canyon in our first-class Pullman train car. Three hours into the heart of the Verde Canyon, we stopped to watch the bald eagles. I was so happy, I felt as if I was soaring with them! After many toasts from our train mates, we arrived back at the station.

The Desert Quail Inn and the Wild Tucan were to provide for the rest of our evening. A week earlier, I had sent copies of each of the most current wedding magazines to the fine people at the inn. This, along with two dozen of the largest white roses in town, were on the coffee table in our suite. The Wild Tucan provided takeout prime rib and wine for dinner. (They even let me borrow their china and flatware!) A dozen long distance phone calls later, we had told the rest of the world of our happiness and upcoming nuptuals! A fire, two-person jacuzzi, and king-size bed helped us end the day as romantically as it had begun. My beautiful bride to be and I will never forget this most special day. *—Amy Theurich & Jeffrey Dillion*

The City of Love

After dating my boyfriend for four years, I began to press the engagement issue. He had wanted to wait until we finished our undergraduate schooling to propose. I wanted him to be romantic, which didn't come naturally at all, and spontaneously propose (early). This past fall, he started discussing wedding plans, like the date or the style of wedding, but he would not propose. One night he took me to a very swanky restaurant that we had never visited before, and then he took me to the campus lake for a moonlight stroll. We held hands and talked about how great things were going. Then, he abruptly said, "It's time to go," and took me home.

There were a series of dates that seemed to be "the night," but it never happened. He traveled with me to my father's house in Florida during Christmas Break. On New Year's Eve, we went to my sister's for a party, and I thought for sure that getting married would be his resolution. At midnight, he kissed me, told me he loved me, and said his resolution was to not make a resolution.

Driving back to Illinois from my father's, Scott suggested a little scenic tour. He wanted to go to New Orleans (which is an eight-hour detour) to eat at Ralph and Kacoo's, a place our friends raved about. He suggested that we arrive in New Orleans at 4 P.M., eat dinner, and drive the remaining ten hours home. While I was not thrilled about the all-night drive, I had wanted to visit New Orleans for a long time. I agreed, but only if he promised to take me again to actually stay in New Orleans. When we arrived, he took me to Ralph and Kacoo's, which was fabulous. Then we walked around the French Quarter. We hopped in a carriage to take a tour, but just as we pulled away from the curb, another couple jumped in and offered to split the fare. Scott was not pleased. While I was in awe of the Big Easy, Scott was looking nervous. Once we finished the tour, he said he wanted to take me to Jackson Square. When we arrived at Jackson Square, it was gated and locked for the night. Scott, the impatient man he is, groaned in agony.

He walked me back to a hotel called the St. Marie. He had made reservations for us! I was so surprised. We went up to the rooms, and found the spacious balcony that overlooked the Quarter and downtown. Just as I turned to look at him, he got on his knees and said, "I have a question to ask you." I said yes before he even got the words out! We spent the weekend strolling through the antique stores, devouring the wonderful food, and being newly engaged.

The greatest thing about his proposal was that he was very romantic and very surprising. The fact that he is not normally that way made it even more special, because I knew he really worked hard at it. He even promised to take me back to New Orleans to celebrate our anniversary. New Orleans may be the Big Easy for most people, but for us, it's the City of Love. —*Kristine Caldwell & Scott Cordts*

Blast from the Past

I awoke at 5:30 A.M. because my fiancé, Phillippe, was walking out of our bedroom door. The thing that struck me as odd was that it was still pitch dark, so I asked him what time it was. He walked over to the alarm clock and said, "Oh, my God! I woke up an hour early!" Then he told me that he was already dressed so he was just going to sit in his office and work on some paperwork. I was very tired and half asleep, so I asked him to call me at 8:30 A.M. to wake me up for work and went back to sleep, not thinking a second thought about it. At 7:04 A.M. I was awakened by a phone call and it was him. Still half asleep, I looked at the clock and asked what he was doing because it wasn't 8:30 yet. He replied, "Wake up, honey, it's going to be a beautiful day!" (which is what my father would say when he woke me as a child). First of all, I thought he had gone nuts, and then I realized that he couldn't be at work because of all the background noise, so I asked him where he was. Of course, he evaded my question and told me to get up and look on the kitchen counter because we had to meet with the past. I got up and went to the counter, where there was a small heart-shaped card and a red rose. In the card was written, "Two years ago, Epiphany

School on Alma Street and Ray around 8 A.M.—remember? Come meet me again. Phillippe."

I got dressed, thinking he was just being romantic and might give me roses and take me to breakfast or something. I had forgotten that it was the anniversary of the day we met until I read the card. We had met for the first time at that school two years prior. I rushed to get dressed because I had to be to work by 10 A.M., and he usually had to be to work by 8:30 A.M. When I finished getting dressed, I woke up my daughter to get her dressed and started to wonder what the heck he was doing—did he realize I had Savanna (my daughter)?

After we were both dressed and ready to go, we got in the car and drove to the school. When I walked towards the room we had taught in together, I saw rose petals sprinkled in a trail down the sidewalk and into the room. As I walked into the room, my favorite song came on— "When We Dance" by Sting—and he pulled me close and walked me to the middle of the room, where there were candles, roses, and a bowl of rose petals and water. He took my hands and said, "Do you remember telling me that it was gonna take a special man to take care of you?" I said yes and he said, "Can I be that person?"

I said, "Yes, of course."

At this point, I still thought he was just being romantic and showing me he loved me, but then he

45

started shaking and his eyes started tearing up as he said, "There's something for you in the water bowl!" I reached in and pulled out my engagement ring, and when I looked up in shock, he asked me to marry him. I said yes.

Throughout the day, he took my daughter and me to places we had visited when we first met—like the first place we ever had lunch together, another school we worked at together, etc. He ended the day by taking me to a restaurant I always wanted to go to called the Top of the Rock, where you eat dinner while viewing the city by candlelight. It was the most beautiful day of my entire life! He even went so far as to wear clothes he was wearing when we first met at the school that morning two years ago. —*Sara Jo Niedelt & Phillippe A. Schneider*

All the News That's Fit to Print

My fiancé, Robin, was doing a production of *Will Rogers' Follies*. At the end of the show, Will received a newspaper and read aloud: "Featured performer in *Will Rogers' Follies* proposes marriage. Stunned girlfriend nearly faints in front of fourteen hundred audience members." The spotlights started to pan the crowd.

I was so excited to find out who the lucky girl was. Will turned to the cast behind him and no one knew what was happening. Finally the lights came to a stop...on me! Robin walked across the stage, looked at me, and said, "I talked to your daddy today and he has given us his blessing." Robin hopped off the stage onto his knee and said, "I would be so honored if you would be my wife." Being an entertainer myself, this was the first time I had ever had stage fright in my life. I looked at my mother, who was just as surprised as I was. She was crying and screaming, "Say yes! Say yes!"

I hadn't said anything, so Robin got off his knee and said, "This is the ring my father used to propose to my mother thirty-eight years ago." I was overwhelmed, but managed to nod yes. The orchestra began to play and Robin swept me up in his arms and carried me down the aisle and out of the theater. —*Sjann Zimmerman*

Cupid Hits His Mark

My fiancé proposed to me on Halloween. I thought that he was working late and really had no idea of his plans, although I knew we would get married someday. I was watching television, hoping that there wouldn't be any trick-or-treaters coming to the door, when his brother called. I was talking to his brother on the phone when I heard the door open. (We live on the top-floor apartment of a house.) Thinking that somebody was opening the door for candy, I jumped off the couch and peered down the dark stairway. I was scared that someone was in the apartment, so I flipped on the light. I caught my fiancé unbuttoning his pants at the bottom of the stairs. I asked him what he was doing and he said, "Don't worry, Honey, I'll be right up." Normally I would have been suspicious but I was still on the phone with his brother, so I turned the light off and went back to the couch. After I hung up the phone, my fiancé jumped into the living room wearing an adult-sized diaper and holding a bow and arrow. I started laughing, thinking that it was his Halloween costume, and he started right into a poem:

"Here I stand dressed as Cupid,
You must think I look real stupid,

Like I belong in a baby carriage,

But I'm here to ask your hand in marriage."

Needless to say, I was doubled over laughing. He pulled a crystal heart-shaped ring box from his diaper and presented me with the ring. "Will you marry me?" he asked.

"Of course!" I replied. It was the best night of my life! —*Marlene Knisley*

The Eager Valentine

My fiancé is not normally a mushy kind of guy, but when it came to our engagement he really got into the romantic stuff. We had been dating for over five years and we had talked about our future together many times, but I was not sure when he was going to ask me and make it official.

A couple weeks before Valentine's Day this year, he told me that he might not be in town that weekend and that maybe we should celebrate early. We planned a romantic dinner at home with wine, candles, and soft music. We also watched the Charlie Brown Valentine's Day special, which we have on tape. It really felt like Valentine's Day even though we were celebrating a week early. After dinner, we exchanged presents. He had gotten me a stuffed pink elephant and a beautiful necklace. Then he said, "I have an extra present for you. Close your eyes and I will be right back."

He left the room for a moment and when he came back he placed the tiny black box in my hand. I think I probably knew instantly what it was, but I opened the box to discover a beautiful solitaire diamond. He took my hands and asked, "Will you marry me?" I started crying before I could even say yes, but was

finally able to answer him. He told me later that the only reason he kept insisting we celebrate Valentine's Day early was because he was so excited that he didn't think he could keep the event a secret for any longer.
—*Jayme Martys*

X-Ray Love

I met Charlie for the first time in the intensive care unit at the children's hospital where he is a physician and I am a dietitian. My heart has never pounded so hard. I remember even feeling light-headed! Little did I know his heart was pounding as hard as mine the first time and every time we saw one another. Charlie was so certain we were made for each other that to get closer to me he conjured up a plan to take a trip to New York City in order to carry out a study on the nutrition of one of his patients. Of course he needed a dietitian (me) to go along since the focus was nutrition. We became best friends working and playing together, somehow knowing in our hearts we were a team for life. Near the end of the trip in Washington Square Park, he kissed me for the first time. Now, seven months later, he is just as spontaneous and romantic as ever. Despite working thirty-six-hour shifts every three nights, not sleeping enough, and trying to sell a house, he found the time to make the day he proposed to me the most special day of my life.

Charlie had told me he had lunch plans with a friend from the hospital and wanted to know if I would like to join them. Taking any chance I get to take a break on a Friday, I went. We went to a quaint, out-of-the-way restaurant with a beautiful view of a rose garden. I remember thinking that for a Friday lunch the place was awfully nice, but of course I had no idea what was coming. After lunch, the friend that had joined us stated she had been taking photography lessons and had a photo on display in a student art center. We went in to view her photo when she stopped and said, "I really like this one." After figuring out the picture was actually an X-ray of a chest with a figure of a ring in the middle of the heart with the hands encasing the heart and ring, I read the engraving below it, which read:

"Title: I Love You Endlessly

Subtitle: Kelly, will you marry me?

Artist: Charlie"

I immediately started bawling as Charlie, barely able to speak, asked, "Kelly, will you marry me?"

After I responded, "Of course I will!" and cried some more, he told me it was his chest in the X-ray and he had taped the ring to his chest (heart) for the picture. Charlie's X-ray expressed to me without words that he's given me his heart forever. I did not believe in love at first sight until I met Charlie. He still makes my heart race every time I see him. We look forward to a lifetime of love and fun together. —*Kelly Kramer*

The Bedtime Story

A year of bliss had come and gone and I thought it was the appropriate time to pop the question. I thought it was too cliché to put a ring in a glass of champagne. Besides...what if she swallowed it? So this is what I did:

Since she has a five-year-old daughter from a previous marriage, I decided to ask while her daughter was there. After all, I would be, in a sense, marrying both of them.

One night when it was time to put her daughter to bed, I told my girlfriend that I had a great bedtime story and wanted her to listen. Coincidentally, it was also Mother's Day eve. Her daughter was in bed, and we both sat on the bed as I began the story.

I told the story of a boy and a girl who lived far, far away from each other. The girl was a princess and had a daughter. One day she was sad so she went for a walk and came upon a fortune-teller named Zelda. She went in and Zelda told her that she would have lots of love, passion, and happiness in her life and that there was a special prince from a far-away land who would help her with this. She felt happy as she left the fortune-teller.

Meanwhile, there was a prince who was also sad and went for a walk. While walking around, he came across a beautiful, shiny black rock. He picked it up and put in his pocket. Then he came across a fortune-teller named Imelda. She said he would some day meet his princess and have lots of love, passion, and happiness.

The prince left the fortune-teller happier than he was, but was still feeling a little sad because he wanted to know who this person was and when he would meet her. So he continued to walk. And he walked and walked and walked. He didn't stop. He walked through rain and forests and jungles. Then one day he looked up and saw a clearing. He went there and saw a beautiful princess playing with her daughter. They looked so happy and fun together.

At first he was quite shy and was intimidated about approaching them. He finally decided to go up to them and introduce himself. He did it in such a funny way that the princess and her daughter laughed and laughed. They seemed to like this new guy, so the princess and her daughter invited him for dinner. They had so much fun together, they invited him to stay there with them.

Several months had gone by, and all three were so happy. So the prince got down on one knee and said, "When I was a little boy, I went to a fortune-teller and she said I would have much love. And when I am with you I do. She said I would have much passion. And when I am with you I do. She said I would have much happiness. And when I am with you I do." So the prince decided to give the princess the only thing he had—that black shiny rock. But when he reached into his pocket the black rock was gone. After all these months the black rock had actually changed.

(At this point I have reached into my pocket and have the diamond engagement ring in my hand.)

So the prince opened up his hand, looked at the black rock that had now become a diamond, and he asked the princess to marry him!

My girlfriend/fiancée was stunned. At that point, her daughter jumped up out of bed and started yelling, "We're getting married! We're getting married! We're getting married!" —*Kit Fedorin & Steve Orloff*

A Cure for Jet Lag

I was in Germany on a business trip when Rob called to remind me that the day after I returned would be our first anniversary. He said he was taking care of the plans and to be prepared to celebrate no matter how jet-lagged I would be. I got in late, but because I was on Germany time I woke up early in the morning. I called Rob and asked him what he had in mind. He told me to be ready by noon and he'd come and pick me up.

The weather was beautiful. We went downtown to all the places we went on our first date one year earlier. Since our anniversary fell on Victoria's Day this year, every place we went was closed, so we just window-shopped. We later went for a walk and had our portrait sketched by a street vendor. It was almost dinnertime by then, so we headed back to the truck.

He wouldn't tell me where we were going for dinner, just that he was pretty sure I'd like it. We drove for a little bit, and then pulled into the CN Tower parking lot. I thought what a great place this was for a special dinner. We went upstairs and had a drink before dinner. By this time I was completely exhausted and didn't think I'd make it through dinner without falling asleep. There wasn't a cloud in the sky and we sat beside the window enjoying the view. You could see all over the city. Then, over Rob's right shoulder, I saw a plane was slowly flying by. There was a banner attached to it, so as he made his way around the tower I read it out loud. It said, "Val will you marry me? Love, Rob." When I got to the "Love, Rob" part I paused. I was going to say, "Isn't that funny, there is another couple here with the same names!" But when I looked over, I saw that he wasn't in his chair. There he was beside me, on his knee, holding a beautiful diamond ring in his hand. He said, "Will you?" I was very jet-lagged and it just didn't click that it was me and this was really happening. So I looked at the plane, looked at Rob, and looked at the ring and slowly added it all up. All I could do was nod my head while he put the ring on my finger. I heard clapping all around us and realized that we had an audience!

He had been planning this the entire week I was away. It was the most amazing moment of my life. I always thought that proposals like that only happened in the movies. I didn't feel the floor beneath my feet as we walked out of the restaurant. Rob is living proof that dreams do come true, because I never thought I'd ever meet someone like him. I do believe I have found my soul mate, and I look forward to spending every minute of our lives together. I can't wait to tell our children the special way their daddy proposed to me. —*Valerie Nicoloff & Robert Van Riel*

The Toe Ring

My fiancée bought a toe ring earlier last summer. Everyone who saw it complimented her on this ring she had on her toe. On her birthday, we had plans to go to a fairly fancy Japanese restaurant in Minneapolis. When I came home from work, she had already been there for an hour or so getting ready.

The first thing I said when I walked through the door was how my toe was hurting all day long and I thought I had an ingrown toenail. She blew it off, knowing that I complain about every little pain.

It was finally time to go. We were walking to our car, which was two or three blocks away from our apartment. Again, I complained about my painful toe. She kept walking, blowing it off again. When we reached the corner of the street, there was a beautiful old Victorian house with a bench at the corner of the sidewalk. I said I couldn't take this any more and that I had to look to see what was wrong. I sat on the bench and took my shoe and sock off with her standing above me looking at me with disgust until she saw the diamond on my "ring" toe.

I asked her if she would marry me. Without any hesitation she said yes—however, there was some laughter.
—*Aaron Pankonin & Charity Sjodin*

Lint...Again?

My boyfriend, Scott, was notorious for playing tricks on me. It seemed that every time we would have a serious conversation about life, love, and children, he would look into my eyes, hold my hand, and tell me that he had something for me. Then, he would reach into his pocket, struggle for a bit and pull out...lint. Yes, lint. It was funny for awhile, but in the back of my mind I wondered if there would ever be a token other than lint.

For my birthday, he asked me to pack my bags for a weekend getaway. Assuming the temperature would be the same as it was in Atlanta, I packed some fall attire—after all, it was December.

Well, when we got to our surprise destination of New Orleans, it was seventy-five degrees. It would have been nice knowing that prior to packing—but how could I complain? Scott had thought of the most romantic weekend of my life—we stayed in a beautiful and romantic hotel in the French Quarter, indulged in the best food and wine New Orleans had to offer, and hung out at smoky after-hour jazz clubs. I couldn't have dreamed of anything better.

On Sunday morning, the day after my birthday, Scott had planned brunch at a restaurant named

Artesia. The town of Abita Springs, where the restaurant was located, was across Lake Ponchartrain—but when we got to the bridge, it was closed due to fog.

Forty-five minutes had passed. My patience was wearing thin, my stomach was growling, and a headache was on its way. At that point, I suggested going to Shoney's or even McDonald's—but just as I spoke, the bridge opened.

When we arrived at Artesia, I was enchanted and amazed by the old plantation house—it felt like I had gone back in time. The branches of a moss-covered tree draped over the Victorian porch where a line of rockers sat. It was truly amazing.

After eating yet another great meal, Scott and I headed outside to the porch, sat back, and enjoyed the captivating setting, fresh air, chilled wine, and, most of all, one another's company.

After a few minutes of conversation, Scott pushed his rocker closer to mine and set down his wine glass. He then turned to me and said, "There's another reason I brought you here this weekend."

I looked at him and saw tears welling in his eye—it looked serious. But I had been tricked before. He then reached in his pocket. Half laughing, half on the verge of tears, I said, "This better not be lint."

Then he pulled out a velvet box. I knew it wasn't a joke this time. As he opened it, I was nearly blinded by the most beautiful, sparkly diamond ring I had ever seen. It was perfect. He had picked it out especially for me. But before he could reach for it, I picked it up and put it on my finger (Emily Post would have shunned me). I was speechless. Actually, I think I was mumbling something like, "I can't believe this is happening," over and over and over. Scott then told me how much he loved me and that he wanted to spend the rest of his life with me.

I smothered him with kisses, and then abruptly I stopped and said, "You still haven't even asked me!"

Scott replied, "Kristi, you haven't given me a chance." We laughed, then he asked, "Will you marry me?"

And my response: "Yes! Yes! Yes!"

We then spent the rest of the day rocking in our chairs, with dumb grins on our faces...just being happy.

And I said, "I wonder if it'll be like this fifty years from now."

Scott said, "It'll be even better." —*Kristin Szuchan & Scott Alpers*

A Real Family

Tom and I have lived together for a little over a year and a half. I have an eight-year-old daughter from a previous marriage, so life has been full of surprises for Tom, who has never been married or had children.

Tom asked my daughter, Chelsey, to start calling him Daddy last Christmas (a major commitment) and we bought a house last month. I didn't expect him to propose because there have been so many changes lately.

On an average Sunday morning, we all went shopping. We came home and hung out a bit together. Then Tom announced that he had bought the wrong thing at the store and needed to exchange it. I thought nothing of it and went back to doing the laundry.

When he came back, I was doing chores and Chelsey was playing outside. He simply sat down on the couch, held my hands and asked if I would marry him and let him adopt Chelsey. He pulled the ring out of his pocket and slipped it on my finger. I cried and accepted. He then asked Chelsey if it was OK with her and she smiled a huge smile. The whole proposal was comfortable, loving, and safe—just like our friendship. Nothing fancy, just life continuing on—and a promise that we will always be a real family.

Forever Flowers

Although my boyfriend and I had been dating for only a few months, we felt as if we had known each other all our lives and that this was the "real thing." It was a long distance relationship, but we spoke every day for over five hours—no small feat considering the three-hour time difference between our locations (Los Angeles and Detroit). This usually meant that one of us was in the middle of something inconvenient when the other one was free. In August, his brother, who lived in Arizona, came to Los Angeles for a conference and we talked about meeting for dinner, but were unable to coordinate our schedules. So he said we should postpone it until the next time he came out to LA, which would be in about a month. About a week later, he called and we set a date: Friday, September 25. He told me that the conference was on Thursday and Friday, and he would bail out on the dinner Friday night to drive out and meet me for dinner. I asked him where his conference was, so that I could give him directions to my house, but he said he didn't know and would get back to me later for directions.

Ten days prior to the twenty-fifth, I received nine long-stemmed exotic peach roses and one long-stemmed red rose with a note from my boyfriend reading, "The first reason I love you is…" with a beautiful, detailed explanation. The next day, I received eight long-stemmed white roses and two long-stemmed red roses, with a note from my boyfriend reading, "The second reason I love you is…" This continued for seven more days, with the number of reasons he loved me corresponding to the number of red roses that I received, and with remaining roses being a different color each day. The number of roses always added up to ten (e.g., on the seventh day, I received seven red roses, three pale pink roses, and the seventh reason that he loved me). All of the roses were exotic breeds and custom-ordered, and my house was starting to smell like a greenhouse. And, he was very creative when telling me the reasons that he loved me. For example, on the seventh day, he sent me a crossword puzzle with clues derived from our relationship (e.g., "three across: the favorite city that we have in common"). Letters in the red squares of the puzzle then had to be unscrambled to form a password. He had left instructions to use the password to open a website that he had created the day before. Upon opening the website, I found the seventh reason he loved me.

In the meantime, he pretended to be jealous that his brother was getting to see me before he would get a chance to fly out again. On the twenty-fifth, the day that I was supposed to meet his brother, the florist called (they had my number because they had been making deliveries for the past nine days) and told me that my flowers would be delayed for a day because they had been special-ordered and were delayed in shipment. I told my boyfriend this and he was angry that the florist had revealed the surprise. I told him that it was OK, that I had guessed I would be getting ten red roses (along with the tenth reason that he loved me) that day anyway. Later in the day, his brother called and told me that he thought it might be best for him, professionally speaking, if he stayed for the postconference dinner, and asked if I would mind joining him there instead. I agreed, and he told me that the conference was at the Hotel Bel-Air in Beverly Hills and that when I arrived I should ask the restaurant manager to show me where the dinner party was. This is exactly what I did, and the manager led me to the foot of the hotel's famous garden, and told me to walk up the hill at the end of the path, where I would find the banquet facilities.

When I began walking up the dark path, what I really found was my six-foot, two-inch fiancé, gorgeous in a tailored Armani suit, holding ten long-stemmed red roses in his hand! He had arranged for his brother to call and set up the dinner, and for the florist to call and tell me the flowers would not be there that day so he could deliver the final ten himself. He then led me to the gazebo, where he had laid out five dozen two-foot long tropical-colored roses in the shape of a heart, along with candles. There was a white metal bench there in the shape of a heart, and he held my hand, sat me down, got on one knee, and told me the tenth reason that he loved me. He then said, "Your love means everything to me. That's why I want to ask you if you'll marry me. So, Anila, will you marry me?" After I whispered yes, he slipped an internally flawless, two-carat, pear-shaped solitaire on my finger. We then sat in the gazebo of the garden, which he had rented for the rest of the evening, and talked about our dreams and plans and all the things we had been waiting for all our lives that we had finally found in each other. Finally, we finished off with dinner at the restaurant of the hotel.

We're planning to honeymoon in Greece and Turkey. My parents adore him, and my teenage brother idolizes him. People ask how I knew that he was "the one" after such a short time, and I tell them that it's because he makes me happier than I have ever been, and that something truly wonderful I did in a past life has been rewarded by this relationship...and that, in the end, is all that really matters. —*Anila Putcha & Ravi Bhagavatula*

A Tropical Surprise

Keith and I had been dating for only a year when I decided to take a trip with my girlfriend Sarah. Keith drove us to the airport in Minneapolis, and walked us to our flight. He kissed me, told me he loved me, and said he would be waiting every night, watching the hands on the clock until I would be home.

Sarah and I got on our plane, and I sat thinking of him and how much I loved him. I already missed him. But this was our long-awaited trip and I owed it to both Sarah and myself to have a great time. We were traveling to the Virgin Islands, a place I had dreamed of going for years. When we arrived, Sarah told me she was exhausted and needed a nap. She went into her room and closed the door, leaving me alone. I figured it would give me a chance to relax and adjust to being without Keith, so I opened the door to my own room. Inside, the floor was covered with tropical flower petals—it looked like a magical fairyland! I followed the signs to the bed and found a small silver box atop satin sheets. Confused, I looked around, but I was alone. Inside the box was a small piece of paper (my stationery from home!) that said, "I've been waiting for this…go to the window."

When I leaned out the window, I couldn't see anything because it was dark. So I leaned out further. To my utter amazement, there was Keith, kneeling in the middle of a throng of my closest friends and relatives! In his hands was a brilliant diamond ring. Everyone I loved was there: they had been planning it for three months, and my trip actually turned out to be a tropical engagement party. I still get shivers up and down my spine when I think about it! I just hope everyone finds someone who makes them feel the way I do when I'm with Keith. It feels so unexplainable to have found my soul mate. —*Willow Gatts & Keith Kraeplin*

Valentine's Day Surprise

On Friday, February 13, I had just finished a long week at work and was very glad to be home. It was our typical Friday evening routine watching television, playing on the computer, and eating pizza. During the evening, my boyfriend told me not to make any plans for Valentine's Day because he had a surprise planned. Later on that evening, he said that he wanted to spend Saturday night on the town, but he had no definite plans as to where we would go or what we would do, so he was looking for suggestions. I was convinced that there would be no Valentine's Day surprises.

On Saturday morning, I gave my boyfriend a heart-felt card. He seemed to be caught off-guard and said what a dog he was because he hadn't actually gone and gotten any kind of acknowledgment of the day for me yet. He said that to make it up to me he would do all of the planning for the evening and would come up with something special. A little later we drove downtown and had a cappuccino and walked around window-shopping without any real definite direction. I dropped a little hint that maybe we could visit some jewelry stores, but my boyfriend pretty much responded as though it was not really a point of interest for him, so

I dropped it, once again thinking there would be no surprises for Valentine's Day that year.

A little while later, he told me that I should plan to be ready for our evening by 4:50 that afternoon. I was somewhat excited; however, I felt that even though a specific time had been stated, our schedule didn't actually have to be strictly followed. But come 5:00, he was standing behind me watching me finish up my hair, looking in a rush. He said, "We have to go right now."

"Just one more minute."

Then the doorbell rang. I was surprised because I wasn't expecting anyone and asked who it was. He just said, "We have to go now."

He proceeded to blindfold me and guide me to the door, telling me that once we got outside, I could not say a word or make any noise. I was really curious now. He directed me into a vehicle and for five minutes we drove in utter silence. Then I heard a slight murmur and my boyfriend told me to take my blindfold off. This was when I discovered that we were in my father's car and my father was driving while my stepmother, in the front seat, was taking off her blindfold as well. I saw we were driving toward the coast; however, we couldn't get a word out of the men as to what was planned.

An hour later, we pulled into the parking lot of a restaurant in a small coastal town. We walked inside and were directed to our table, where two huge bouquets of a dozen long-stemmed red roses were sitting on the table waiting for us. All the ladies in the restaurant were looking at us like we were the luckiest girls in the world, while all the men in the restaurant looked a little agitated that this display of affection was stepping up their date's expectations of them for the evening. We ordered wine and dinner and ate, drank, and talked. My Valentine's Day had been made complete. The waitress came back to clear our plates and we ordered dessert. After she left, my boyfriend turned to my father and said he was really glad it was Valentine's Day because he wanted to tell me (he than turned in my direction) he was really glad I was his Valentine and that he wanted to make me his Valentine for life. He got down on one knee and pulled out a box and opened it to reveal a perfect ring and asked me if I would marry him. It was then I realized that, despite the fact that my father and my boyfriend had conspired behind our backs to plan the special evening, this part of the plan had not been shared between the two men. With my father smiling and crying in surprise and tears coming to my eyes as well, my boyfriend slipped the ring on my finger as I said, "Yes, yes, yes!" It was the best Valentine's Day I ever had. —*Holly Cavin & Dana Olden*

Storybook Love

Jason and I met at church this summer. Our church has been the backbone of our relationship and the location for many of our special moments. For example, he first asked me on a date at church and we had our first dance in the parking lot.

He brought me to church under false pretenses and surprised me by bringing me into the sanctuary where two chairs were turned to face each other. Those chairs were the chairs we were sitting in when he first asked me on a date. At our feet was a Creative Memories photo album in red (my favorite color). I thought nothing of it because he had been telling me he had a present for me.

Jason put the album together with very little help from others and spent hours making it special. The album was filled with pictures of us as we grew up, of our families, and of our friends. The album then continued into a written story illustrated by our pictures. It told a story of a little boy who dreamed of meeting that special girl one day, and a little girl who dreamed of meeting that special boy one day. The little boy grew up and eventually accepted Jesus in his heart and God began to prepare him for the skills he would someday need to be a husband. At the same time, that little girl was accepting Jesus and being prepared by God with the skills she would need to be a wife.

One day the little boy met the girl at church and eventually asked her to go on a date. She said yes and they talked for hours after dinner. They fell in love and the little girl began to wonder when they would get married. Then one day the boy took the girl to church, he got down on his knee, took her hands, and asked her to share the rest of her life with him…

We were both crying and I immediately said yes. It was more than I ever dreamed of and it was planned around all the things that I hold dear. —*Jessi Perron & Jason Hackenmueller*

The One and Only

It was a perfect winter day in Buffalo. There was quite a bit of snow on the ground, but the sun was shining, creating the image of tiny diamonds glistening off its surface.

My fiancé woke me up early in the morning and said he was feeling kind of down and wanted to go to the cemetery to visit his grandfather, who had passed away two years earlier. Because my fiancé and his grandfather were so incredibly close, I would never hesitate to make time for him to mourn his lifelong friend. So we went to a nearby florist and picked up a Christmas wreath to place before the headstone.

Once we arrived, I let him spend time there alone for a couple of minutes and remained in the car. At that moment, I thought to myself, "Look at him, so beautiful and the scenery so beautiful, it looks like a portrait. His head bowed, tears falling from his eyes, thinking of how much he misses the person responsible for his being here two generations ago, and how much he has grown up to love this man that must have played such an integral part in his character." I wanted to cry myself.

Then I stepped out of the car and went by him and said a prayer, because I too loved this man so much for playing a part in making my fiancé who he was, although I only had the pleasure of knowing him three short years.

After a few moments, my fiancé turned to me and said, "Sometimes I am so sad that I waited so long to ask you this, because I wish my grandfather were here to hear me say these words: Will you marry me?" I started to cry, and he went on to say that no matter who crossed his path in life, I would be the one person who would truly understand the deep feelings he holds in his heart for his grandfather. So, although he knew it seemed crazy, he wanted to be here where he felt closest to his grandfather. And, he knew he didn't have to explain this to me because I am the one person in the world that truly understands. He really wanted to be there with his two best friends. "I love you, Lisa," he said and kissed me, and, at that moment, I knew that no matter what happened between us I would also always remain special in his heart, and there would be no one else that would ever truly understand his feelings. I was so happy he asked me there.

Of course I said yes, but I was hysterically crying at the time. It seems funny to say that my fiancé asked me to marry him in a cemetery, but you would have to have been there to understand. I wouldn't have wanted it any other way. —*Lisa Marie Demont & Ronald Bolognese*

The Magic Trick

Brian and I had been going out for quite some time. We had just moved in together and decided to throw a party. Brian had recently taken up magic and was getting very good at it. We decided our party would be a barbecue and magic show. We invited both our families and some of our close friends. We were expecting about thirty people to be at the party, which was to be in the recreation room of our apartment complex.

Three days before the party, I received a call from the apartment office. They asked how many guests we were planning on having, and I told them about thirty, and was then informed that the maximum occupancy for the room was ten. The lady on the phone was very apologetic but said there was nothing she could do. We would have to find another place to have our party. I was not very happy, but when I told Brian he went through the roof. We were having relatives from out of town come and everything. Brian went right down to the office to talk to them. About fifteen minutes later he was back with no success. It was an insurance issue—their insurance only covered ten people, and that was that. Luckily Brian's parents don't live too far away and let us have it in their backyard instead.

The day of the party finally came and all was going very well. Then it was time for the magic show. Brian had been working very hard and I was a little nervous because he had never performed his magic in front of so many people. Everyone loved it and they were very impressed by his talent. Throughout the show he had members from the audience come up and help. But I was very surprised when, during his last trick, he asked for a volunteer and wanted me to come up there. We had not talked about this before, but I went up there anyway.

He needed a ring for this trick, so he asked me to remove one of mine. He said he was going to clean it. He wrapped it in tissue paper and put it in a small silver bowl. He then struck a match and put it in the bowl also. There was a big flame and he snuffed it out with the lid. When he took the lid off he was already apologizing because he knew my ring must be ruined. Inside the bowl was a small packet of tissue paper. He handed it to me and asked if it was my ring. It was a ring all right, but it was not the ring I had given him. It was a beautiful diamond solitaire engagement ring! As I unwrapped it, Brian got down on one knee. He told me I was his best friend and that he couldn't see his life without me in it and asked if I would marry him. Of course, that last part is not verbatim because by this time I was sobbing uncontrollably with joy, but I said yes!

For the finale he made it snow (in July) while he played "Beth" by Kiss in the background. He is a romantic at heart and that is one of the reasons I love him. He not only caught me off-guard, but most of our friends and family did not know that it was going to be an engagement party! —*Beth Smith & Brian Poindexter*

A Country and Western Proposal

I met my fiancé, Victor, a little over a year ago in a beginning country and western dance class. I was a first-time student and he was the instructor. Victor and I quickly became friends and spent many nights out on the town practicing our dance moves. We eventually fell head over heels in love. Victor proved himself to be the most loving, caring, affectionate man I have ever met.

Two weeks ago, Victor and I were on our way to a surprise birthday party for one of our friends. Little did I know that Victor had no intention of actually going to the party—it was all a setup to throw me off-guard. I also had no idea that my good girlfriend, Michele, was in my apartment packing my bags at that very moment for our surprise weekend getaway!

As we were driving to the party, Victor suggested that we stop off at a restaurant for a drink first since we were running a little early. It just so happened to be the restaurant where he took me on our first date. While we were inside, my friend Michele drove to the restaurant and dropped off my packed bags in the trunk of Victor's car. We had a good time at the restaurant and laughed as we reflected back on our first date. We left the restaurant and began to drive to the party. Before I knew it, Victor had taken a detour and wound up at the airport! When we arrived at the terminal, there stood Victor's roommate ready to jump in the car and take off. But first, Victor unloaded our bags from the trunk. I stood there in amazement as I realized what was taking place. Victor gave me a big hug and said "I'm taking you away for the weekend. You've been working way too hard with your new job!"

Victor made me wait in the lobby as he checked in for the flight. We made our way down to the gate, but he wouldn't tell me where we were going. Because of the crowd at the airport and the close proximity of the gates, it wasn't until we were up in the air that I found out where we were going.

We arrived in Austin, Texas, and eventually found the bed and breakfast where Victor had made reservations. It was nestled in the heart of the city up on a hill on two acres of land overlooking the skyline of Austin. It was so quaint and absolutely beautiful! In the backyard there was a pool, a gazebo, a hot tub, and beautiful rolling green hills.

The next day we woke up and drove around Austin sightseeing. We made it back to the hotel around 4 P.M. and decided to take a nap before we went out to dinner. We were both very excited about checking out the country and western dance clubs in Austin. When I awakened two hours later, Victor was gone. In the room were two dozen roses, a lit candle, and a card sitting beside the candle. The note said, "Take a shower, get dressed, and meet me out by the gazebo."

When I had finished dressing, I walked down along the winding path toward the gazebo. When I arrived, I noticed Victor was dressed very handsomely. There was a table set up with candles, a bottle of wine, and two glasses, and music playing on a portable CD player. He smiled at me, took my hand, and asked me to dance. It was so romantic! After we finished dancing, he asked me to sit down. He began to tell me why and how much he loved me. He then put on another song that told a story about a man proposing to his girlfriend. I cried as I realized what was about to happen.

Victor then got down on one knee, pulled out a beautiful diamond ring, and started singing the song to me. At that moment he proposed and I said yes! He then pulled a small tape recorder out of his front pocket and said, "This is for the benefit of our future children— so they too can relive the night their father proposed to their mother." He began to describe into the microphone the beautiful surroundings and everything he had done the past two months to prepare for this moment. —*Alexia Pearce & Victor Arboleda*

The Scavenger Hunt

My fiancé, Pete, and I live in New York City. He planned his proposal for months, eventually letting all of our friends and family in on the upcoming engagement, including asking my parents for their blessing on Christmas Eve. In March, he executed his plan.

Pete had devised a bogus scavenger hunt around New York City, supposedly sponsored by a major credit card company, and had enlisted a friend from my office, Linda, to invite me to go on the hunt with her. We were "teammates," with Linda being the "team captain."

Linda and I hiked all around Manhattan (in the rain), picking up riddles at various locations, such as Macy's, St. Patrick's Cathedral, and Penn Station. Each riddle we solved led us to our next location and our next riddle. For example, at St. Pat's, we received the riddle, "Head to the New York City location named after the Keystone State and claim your next clue from the bag people." This led us to Penn Station, to the Amtrak Baggage Claim, where we picked up an actual piece of luggage with our next clue inside.

The final riddle led us to our "Master Destination," Tavern on the Green in New York's Central Park, where there was supposedly a cocktail reception and award ceremony to end the scavenger hunt. Yet another package was picked up at the restaurant, instructing the "shortest person on the team" to go to the gift shop to pick up their invitation to the award ceremony, and the "tallest person on the team" to go outside to the carriage marked with an X to pick up an invitation. Linda is five feet, four inches tall and I am five feet, eight inches tall, so I headed out to the carriage.

Walking toward the only horse-drawn carriage there, I started wondering if this was the big moment. The last clue seemed a little odd and sounded like something Pete would do. The driver opened the canvas door to the carriage and there was Pete, all dressed up, offering his hand and asking me to come inside. I was in shock. He got down on one knee and said, "I love you more than words and riddles can express. I intend for our life together to be a never-ending adventure. Will you marry me?" He was crying, I was crying, but his shaking hands somehow got the ring on my shaking finger, and we took a romantic carriage ride through Central Park.

The day was far from over, though. The carriage let us out at a restaurant adjacent to the park where we had reservations for dinner. We started up the stairs to our table on the second floor, and stopped halfway, where Pete said to me, "You know how much I love you, right?" I understood what he meant when we reached the top of the stairs and our parents were sitting at our table. Pete had arranged for his parents, who are from Long Island, to pick up my parents, who are from Wisconsin, at the airport the previous night. Pete had secretly flown them in to celebrate the day with us. It had always been both of our wishes to have our parents nearby when the big day happened.

The best day of my life ended with a stay at the Waldorf-Astoria Hotel. Pete had our room stocked with red roses, bridal magazines, and strawberries.

Pete put so much effort and thoughtfulness into our engagement. I know the rest of our lives together will be just as special as our engagement day. —*Kristin Sorensen & Peter Campisi*

A Messy Proposal

My engagement story is not only funny, but rather on the messy side.

My fiancé decided that he wanted to go hiking on a Sunday morning at a large park with many hiking trails. The hiking spot he picked was about an hour away. So we got on the highway and headed toward the park. After about an hour and a half I had finally asked him if we were getting close and he said that he actually didn't recognize any of the highway signs we were passing. I was driving, but I had never been to this park, so I had no idea where we were going. It turned out that we had gotten on the wrong highway and were driving in the opposite direction of where we wanted to go. Anyone that knew my fiancé would know that he was not thinking straight at all that day. He is such an avid traveler and knows his way around anywhere he goes.

We got to the park much later that day. It turned out that most of the trails could not be used because of heavy rains the previous week. We went anyway. The whole time we were walking he would not let me walk on his right side and I hadn't the slightest clue why.

We eventually stopped near the edge of a river that flows through the park. He was behind me and when I turned around he was on his knee in the mud. But he had gotten a little too close to me on his knee and when I turned around I fell into him and we fell into the mud on the riverbank—ring and all. I didn't care much about the mud, I was so happy that he asked me to marry him. Since we have been dating for over five years, I never thought this day would come. *—Amy Maloney & Scott Bretthaver*

Message in a Bottle

Brian and I had been dating for about a year and a half and I had begun to accept the fact that we would probably never get married—he was a die-hard bachelor. On the first day of our vacation last week, things were not looking good. We drove all night, didn't get any sleep, and were both wearing thin on each other. When we finally got to the condo, I realized that I had left my bathing suits in the truck! Brian had been fussing about all the luggage I brought and refused to go get my bathing suits for me. I was furious, because I had already undressed. About a minute later, he rushed into the bedroom and said that he didn't mind getting my suits for me and that he would be right back. About forty minutes later, he walked in holding a drink. I about lost it because I had been waiting so long and I thought he had been down there the whole time flirting with the beautiful bartender at the pool. I even made some stupid jealous comment about it.

Because it was late and we were both tired, we decided to take a nap and made dinner reservations for 7:30 that night. I woke up around 6:40 and woke Brian up. He rushed into the bathroom and starting taking a shower. When he got out he started rushing me, telling me that I had to be ready by 7:00. I hate to be rushed, and besides, I had heard him make the reservation for 7:30! He was actually standing behind me snapping his fingers! I got so mad that I just said, "Whatever! I'll be ready in five minutes!" I didn't even take a shower or anything.

Finally, when we got downstairs he said, "Why don't we take a quick walk on the beach?"

"What?" I yelled, "You just rushed me to take a walk on the beach?"

But I was tired of fussing, so I gave in. We were walking along the beach when Brian said, "Look, there's something on the beach."

It was a wine bottle, and I said, "Someone probably just left it there." As we got closer, I noticed that it had a piece of paper in it. Being the kid that I am, I got really excited and ran over to it to try to get the paper out. It was a treasure map! At the bottom it had an arrow that said "Turn over." On the other side it said, "Will you marry me? I love you! Brian James Hollis 6-13-98." I said it all out loud and then said, "What? Will you marry me?"

When I turned around, he was on one knee with the most beautiful ring in the world in his hand. I was so shocked that I couldn't even talk. I had no clue whatsoever! A whole group of people instantly walked up and started to congratulate us. They had tried to pick up the bottle earlier but the lifeguards were guarding it, so they were all waiting around to see what would happen. As it turned out, that's why he was gone so long when he went to get my bathing suit earlier! Boy, did I eat my words! As far as I was concerned, Brian had hung the moon! I am looking forward to a wonderful and exciting life with him! —*Kerry Rich & Brian Hollis*

The Seven Gifts

Here is the story of the most incredible, unimaginable, romantic experience of my life…

I awoke Saturday morning to my sister tapping my shoulder, telling me my boyfriend of seven years, Kenny, wanted me to read a note. The note read something like this: "I wanted to remind you how truly wonderful life can be, so wake up! You have an exciting day planned for you! Amy Starr will arrive at 10 to help you pack. I love you—have fun today!"

I knew, then and there, I was getting engaged! When my friend arrived, we loaded up the car for a trip I'll never forget.

After I asked what felt like a million unanswered questions, Amy finally passed me a note, which read: "Go to the first place we met and a present you will get."

Off I went to the apartment complex where we met. I found a wrapped CD with our song "Piano Man." This is our song because I attended Oregon State University in Portland, and Kenny would ride the train from Seattle (my hometown) to Portland to meet me for the weekends. We'd stop at this piano bar at the train station each time he'd visit and throw our request—"Piano Man"—into the fishbowl.

I was onward bound with a new note: "I hope by now you get the gist, now go to the place where we first kissed." Off I went to the restaurant, where a bag full of Hershey's Kisses awaited my arrival!

I got back into the car with a new note: "I hope you're having fun, you're almost through, now go to the place I first said I love you!" (In actuality, the adventure wasn't almost through—it was just beginning!)

The next item to be handed to me wasn't a note, but a train ticket to Portland. It was my turn to take the train! As we neared the station, I was a little upset that I was taking the trip alone. Then my friend eased my mind with a second train ticket and a note, which read: "I knew you would get bored although Portland's not far, so for this trip you get to bring Amy Starr!"

I sat on the train, emotionally exhausted from the fantastic day. I was nervous and excited because I thought I knew what was ahead! I didn't.

The first stop was Tacoma. To my surprise, another of my best friends boarded the train with a card and a gift! Next stop was Olympia, then it was Longview, then Kelso. At every stop I received another card, another gift, and another friend. We all laughed and we all cried—it was incredible. When we arrived in Portland, my knight in shining armor was there to greet me at the train station, just as I had done for him so many times years ago!

We said good-bye to my girlfriends and set off to the Benson Hotel, a historic beautiful building in downtown Portland. We were late for the romantic dinner he had planned, so we just dropped our bags and turned to run out the door, and it was then that he popped the question. I was overwhelmed by the thought, the time, and the energy he had put into this event, and I was so in love looking at him on his knee! Of course I said yes, through blurred vision.

The restaurant, which is called McMenamins, was beautiful with its old brick buildings and spectacular gardens. We even got lucky with a sunny evening.

As we entered the restaurant, I couldn't believe my eyes—we were receiving a standing ovation from everyone in the restaurant! Most importantly, I looked into the faces of twenty or so of our best friends! They had all traveled the three and a half hours from Seattle to Portland to surprise me with an engagement party!
—*Courtnie Lamb & Ken Williams*

Shopping Spree

One day a girlfriend of mine called and asked me if I wanted to go to the mall to shop for awhile. We walked into the mall and the first shop we went into was a shoe store. I saw a pair black sandals that I liked. She talked me out of buying them.

Our next store was a clothing store. I saw a wonderful two-piece silk pant set. Once again, she talked me out of buying it.

She then told me that she needed to find a jewelry store because she needed to look at some earrings. While in the store she suggested that we look at some rings. I saw the most wonderful diamond ring I'd ever seen. Well, she didn't have to talk me out of that one because I knew that I simply couldn't afford it. We ended up leaving the mall empty-handed.

When I returned home, my boyfriend (now fiancé) had a nice candlelit dinner waiting for me. After dessert, he went back into the bedroom and came back with a gift-wrapped box. It was relatively large, so I knew that it couldn't be a ring. I opened it and there was that pair of black sandals that I saw in the mall. He told me to go back in the bedroom and try them on. When I made it back to the bedroom I saw another box.

It was the two-piece silk pant set that I had liked. I saw where this was leading, so I immediately got excited. I tried on the outfit and the shoes and waited for the other, but nothing else came. I finally gave up.

That night, while I was taking a shower, he snuck in the bathroom and stood on top of the toilet to see over the shower curtain. He startled me when he threw the ring box over the curtain and said, "I love you with all of my heart and I want to spend not only the rest of my life with you, but also eternity. Will you marry me?" I started to cry and said yes with no regrets.

I found out later that night that he had followed me to the mall with my best friend (she was also in on the whole thing), and as I walked out of each store, he walked in behind me and purchased each item I'd seen and wanted. —*Tiffany Toliver & Charles Bates*

Love at First Sight

After being divorced and raising three boys to adulthood, I had vowed that I would never remarry. I had dated a lot, and was very happy with the single life and being independent. A friend from work kept trying to introduce me to Sam, a forty-four-year-old bachelor who just wanted someone to be able to wine and dine. After exhausting every excuse, I finally agreed to go to her house at the lake for the day while Sam was in town visiting. Yes, there is love at first sight. We spent a wonderful day swimming in the lake, then shared a grilled dinner with drinks, and finished the evening watching the sun set and the moon rise over the lake from the deck.

I went home feeling like I had just spent the most wonderful vacation of my life in a matter of hours. We didn't even kiss. The following day, I received a call asking me to come back to the lake for the afternoon and I was more than happy to go.

Three days later I was celebrating my birthday at work, when a beautiful arrangement of flowers was delivered with a simple card that said 'Sam'.

We met for dinner the next week and he returned to our little town the following weekend. A group of us went to a dance and when Anne Murray's "Can I Have This Dance (for the Rest of My Life)" played, he said, "Can I?"

But it was not to go quite that fast. Two months later, my parents were visiting from Florida. Sam wanted to go to the mall, where he purchased my engagement ring, while I cried. He carried the ring home, and when my parents arrived that evening, he asked them if he could have my hand. My mother, being silly, said yes, but you must take the rest of her too. Sam proceeded to get down on one knee, proposed, and slipped the ring on my finger. My eighteen-year-old was so happy that he cried for us.

Yes, there is love at first sight, and yes, you can find happiness in your forties! —*Llewellyn Brannen & Salvatore DiMisa*

Meant to Be

Every summer since I can remember, my family has gone to Myrtle Beach, South Carolina, for vacation. Like any typical summer, my family drove there from Connecticut in July 1988. I was sixteen years old then, and I met a fifteen-year-old girl named Cheryl from Virginia. We hung out together the entire week that we were there, talking about boys and what our futures might bring. We got along so well that we decided to become pen pals. So, for the next six years, we wrote back and forth to each other.

In 1994, I sent Cheryl a letter telling her that I was moving to Virginia, about fifteen miles away from her. She responded with enthusiasm, and told me that she wanted to fix me up with her boyfriend's brother, Bob. Well, for the couple of months before I moved, I kept thinking about my date with Bob, and my new life in Virginia. I finally moved to Virginia and met Bob on a double date with Cheryl and Bob's brother, Pete. We hit it off instantly. I came home from our first date, and told my roommates that this was the guy that I was going to marry—no doubt about it!

We continued to date for another three and a half years, during which Cheryl and Pete were married. The summer of 1998 was coming up, and my family, Bob, and I were heading to Myrtle Beach as usual. This year, Pete and Cheryl decided to join us. Cheryl and I were very excited to be back in Myrtle Beach together, where "everything" started. The second night that we were there, Bob took me for a walk on the beach in the moonlight. It was beautiful; the waves were crashing against the shore and a warm breeze was blowing. Bob stopped and took my hands and said, "Do you realize that this is the ten-year anniversary of when you met Cheryl right here on this beach? I guess that means that we'll be here with them ten years from now with our children." Then he bent down and drew a huge heart in the sand, got down on one knee in the middle of it, and asked if I'd marry him. Of course, I was thrilled and said yes!

Bob said he had a lot of opportunities to propose during the past few months, but he wanted to wait until we were in Myrtle Beach, where it all began. So, little did we know when we were fifteen and sixteen, laying on the beach in 1988, living hundreds of miles apart, that Cheryl and I would grow up to marry brothers! —*Jennifer Welch & Robert Lackey*

Diving for Diamonds

On our yearly trip to Sea World of Ohio, we went to watch the "Pearl Divers"—an exhibit where young girls demonstrate the age-old Japanese tradition of diving for oysters. We had purchased pearls here on previous visits as souvenirs of the day, so I was clueless as to what was about to happen.

On this day, the girl was talking about the history and asked for a volunteer from the audience; my boyfriend raised his hand, so she called both of us on the small stage. The diver swam to the bottom of the pool and pulled an oyster up and handed it to the oyster "shucker," who in turn cracked the shell as we had seen done many times before. However, this time there was no oyster, nor was there a pearl. Inside this shell was a very special gift—a beautiful diamond ring!

My boyfriend then got down on one knee in front of my family (who had been hiding behind a Japanese screen) and a bunch of strangers who were just as shocked as I was, and asked me to be his wife. Of course I said yes! —*Tracy Howard & Arnie Grygorcewicz*

Dr. Belly Button

I proposed to my fiancée, Beckie, on the anniversary of our first date. She is a doctor doing her first year of residency in pediatrics. For several months prior to the proposal we had done some casual ring shopping, so I could get an idea of what she liked. Once I had a general idea, I designed an engagement ring (I'm no artist, but I'm artistic) and had a family friend in New York create it for me. The ring was shipped to me only two days before the engagement—it was beyond my wildest expectations!

Two weeks before I proposed, I suggested to Beckie that I'd like to celebrate our anniversary by going back to the restaurant we went to on our first date (The Cheesecake Factory—yummy!). I also began strongly suggesting that this was going to be a very special night. She later told me that she picked up on this message and the importance I seemed to be putting on this special night.

What she didn't know was that I had been conspiring with the doctors and residents she worked with at the hospital for several months already, and that she would be surprised with a proposal at a lunchtime "meeting" rather than at dinner. Here's how I did it...

I had the director of her residency program call a fictitious mandatory meeting for all the residents and medical students. I then set up a video camera in the corner of the conference room and hid in the back corner of the room with a lab coat on and several others blocking Beckie's view of me. A seat was saved for her in the front row by a friend who said she wanted to talk to her during lunch. Beckie was escorted in by the program director, who had intercepted her before the meeting to make sure she came in when everything was ready. So far, so good...she didn't suspect a thing!

As a final touch, I recruited the help of a four-year-old patient who has a special rapport with "Dr. Beckie." Every time she sees this patient, Beckie goes on a "belly button hunt." Knowing this, I arranged for a nurse to bring her patient to the meeting after her treatment because she wanted to see "Dr. Beckie." When this adorable little girl was wheeled in, Beckie played her role perfectly by going for the belly button. But when she lifted up the shirt, she found the jewelry box taped to the little girl's tummy. Beckie didn't quite know what to make of it, and hesitated for a moment. At that same moment, I snuck up to the front of the room with a dozen roses and said loudly, "Hey Dr. Belly Button, aren't you going to look in the box?"

Beckie turned, saw me, and the first words out of her mouth were, "Oh, God!" At that point, I got down on one knee, asked her if she would marry me, and was rewarded with a quiet yes and a hug and kiss. I was still holding the roses, so Beckie placed the ring on her own finger!

One of the medical students in the back then asked whether she'd said yes. When I responded that she had, the whole room of around thirty to forty people broke out in applause. As icing on the cake, she was given the rest of the day off, and we spent the rest of the day spreading the news amongst our families and friends. I cannot express how deeply I am in love with this wonderful woman, or how much I look forward to our upcoming wedding! —*Rebecca Bezman & Stephen Bergman*

The Birthday Knight

My boyfriend woke me up early on the day of my twenty-sixth birthday and handed me a blank three-ring notebook with the words "Tracey's 26th Birthday" written across the top. He told me it was my job that day to fill the book up. With that, he handed me a disposable camera and told me to get in my car, turn on a particular radio station and drive to New Haven. He gave me no other instructions. I thought he was coming with me, but he was not.

Confused, I got in my car and started driving. My car phone rang and my brother's voice came over the line, instructing me to look in my glove box. I did, and there was the first page of the book with a poem and directions to my destination. I arrived at a day spa where I got a massage, manicure, and facial. As I was about to leave, a woman handed me another page to the book with a poem and instructions to my next destination. This was getting fun!

I arrived at two boutiques, where there were presents and pages waiting with the salespeople. I was instructed to go to my boyfriend's restaurant (he is a chef), where my best friend was waiting. We had lunch and he produced another page.

I then was sent to my mother's house, where she was waiting. She handed me another page and it sent me home. A dress was waiting for me. I knew the evening would end with dinner. I certainly did not expect a proposal on my birthday—he was too clever for that. Another page with a poem was under my car mat as we drove to dinner. It asked me to wish upon the first star I saw.

We went to dinner at a beautiful bed and breakfast. I expected that he would end the evening by telling me that we were staying overnight. Tim disappeared to the bathroom at dessert time. I saw the waitress approaching with another page. I thought it was going to say that he was waiting for me upstairs. It read "All your life you have waited for your knight in shining armor to come into your life—turn around to meet your knight so he can make you his wife." There he was kneeling in full armor, holding the ring. My knight had come! Of course I said yes between the laughter and tears of how funny he looked in black tights. What is funnier is that he had stripped in the parking lot to put on this suit of armor!

There was Intrigue. Action. Adventure. And, of course, Romance.

It all started at 9 A.M. My fiancé, Josh, told me we had to help some friends move. We were both complaining about the early hour, and the fact that our friends never had real sugar to put in their coffee. So we decided to stop at a mini-mart to get a cup of coffee before lugging boxes up and down stairs.

He rolled his car through the red light at the end of his street (I always yell at him about that), and wouldn't you know it—lights started flashing from behind us.

Josh cursed and pulled into an empty parking lot. The police car blocked us in between a deserted building and the street, so we had nowhere to move. As we were waiting for the officer to approach, I noticed Josh shaking uncharacteristically, as if he was in real fear of getting in trouble with the law.

After three or four minutes of letting us "sweat it out," the unsmiling officer came to the driver's window and asked Josh for his license and registration. As Josh handed over the information, the officer scowled. He took the license and registration back to his car.

In the meantime, another police car had pulled up. The two policemen conferred for what seemed like forever (it was really only about ten minutes). While they were talking, I put on my lap belt and made sure Josh did the same.

The officers returned to the car and told us that Josh's license was suspended because he failed to pay some tickets. Josh looked bewildered because he is conscientious about that sort of thing. While I was racking my brains to figure out when this could have happened, the officers asked Josh to step out of the car. I asked if I should get out, too, and the larger officer said, "Yes. Stand over there by the police car, but stay close because I don't want to have to chase you down."

Now, I understand that policemen in the city have to be careful, but I was getting really nervous when they started to frisk Josh. They asked him if he had any weapons or sharp objects in his pants, and didn't seem to believe him when he said no.

After searching Josh thoroughly, they asked him to stand over by me while they searched the car. It seemed like they were expecting to find some contraband.

After a minute or so of rummaging around, one officer called to the other and said, "Hey, look at this!"

I almost had a heart attack. I was thinking of how Josh betrayed me, and wondering what was in his car that would cause the police to become agitated?

One of the policemen stepped away from the car with something in his hand and a grim look on his face. He said, "Can you explain this?"

Josh, looking nervous, said, "Yes I can, Officer." And then he walked up to the policeman, took the object out of his hand, walked over to me, staring me straight in the eyes, got on one knee, and said, "Kris, you are the most beautiful person I've ever met. I love you now and forever. Please be my wife."

I couldn't speak. The cop said, "You have to say something now."

But I couldn't. I just looked at the ring in Josh's hand, started to cry and hugged Josh until I could gain enough control over myself to say, "Of course I will."

Josh started whooping, jumping up and down (with me still in his arms), and screaming, "She said yes! She said yes!" The police officers patted him on the back and hugged me. My heart was still pounding ten minutes later, and I asked one of the officers if he thought I would endure any long-term heart problems!

So all in all, it was a nerve-racking, but wonderful day. I can't say that I was totally enthused with the excessive use of police officers (I think one would have been enough), but I will say this: for the rest of the day, I kept telling Josh, "Run through that stop sign. I want more jewelry!"

A Full (Monty) Proposal

My fiancé, Milind, wanted to propose in an original way. And, boy did he!

We had recently been to see *Titanic* and I mentioned how wonderful I thought he would look in the white tie and tail combo you see all through the movie. I thought it would be awhile before I would see him in one, though. I was wrong.

One Saturday morning, Milind announced he had a surprise for me. He returned shortly from the bedroom dressed in the white tie and tails combo, complete with top hat and cane. I was so surprised that it didn't occur to me to wonder why he was dressed like this—until he turned on the stereo. "Hot Stuff" by Donna Summer filled my ears as he began a *Full Monty*-style striptease. By the end, I was laughing hysterically and he was standing before me wearing nothing but a strategically placed top hat. In the next instant, he was down on one knee, pulling the most beautiful and perfect engagement ring out from behind the hat and asking me to do the honor of marrying him. I shrieked, "Of course!" in delight and the rest is history. *—Gretchen Dougherty & Milind Shah*

Diamonds in the Snow

On Valentine's Day he told me to dress warm—we were going snowshoeing in Rocky Mountain National Park. After tripping over ourselves and having a few snowball fights, he led me to a beautiful rock next to a frozen waterfall overlooking the whole mountain range. After we ate a wonderful meal he had made, he started telling me how wonderful the last year had been. But when he dropped to a knee to propose, he had trouble getting the ring out of his snow pants—I guess his hands were shaking too much. I was very excited, and I guess so was he. In his hurry, the ring box popped open and the ring went sailing. I thought it had gone over the steep cliff. He was still down on one knee with an absolute look of panic, not knowing what to do.

After a moment, in a squeaking voice he said, "Um, hang on one second." He had seen the ring plunge into a snowbank about fifteen feet away. After a minute of awkward digging he returned to a knee and said, "Let's try this again." Then he asked me to marry him. He took me out to a wonderful restaurant and when I got home my room was completely filled with beautiful flowers. It wasn't exactly how I always imagined it, but it will always be my favorite memory.

A Late-Night Phone Call

My fiancé and I live very far apart—he lives in Idaho and I live in Manitoba. One night I went to bed early and had just fallen asleep when my roommate woke me up, saying that Mike was on the phone and had to talk to me right away. I got up, stumbled down to the telephone in the sitting room, and picked up the telephone. Mike said that he was feeling a little nervous. I assumed that he was feeling antsy about living so far apart and began to reassure him. After a few minutes, he excused himself. I was waiting patiently for him to pick up the phone again when I felt a tap on my shoulder. Mike was standing right behind me! After I finished hugging him, he got down on one knee, told me that he could not live without me, and asked me to marry him.

My roommates and parents had known about him flying up all along. My father picked him up at the airport and my roommate gave the signal (the porch light being off) when I went to bed. Another friend called the house, then Mike picked up the extension while my roommate went upstairs to call me to the phone.

This was the most romantic and thrilling moment of my life. To top it all off, my roommate had also arranged for me to have the next day off from work!

The First Pitch

Atlantic City had just opened a minor league baseball stadium, so my boyfriend made plans for the two of us and his parents to go see a game. During the second inning, a PR person with the Atlantic City Surf came over and informed me that my seat was chosen to throw the first ball at the third inning and they would return to get me. Meanwhile, I was so nervous because I have no athletic ability at all and was totally embarrassed that I had to go out on the mound and throw a ball in front of four thousand people. Of course, his parents thought it was great.

At the middle of the second inning, they came back to get me and informed me that if I threw the ball and it made it to the catcher I would receive two free game tickets. At the beginning of the third inning, the announcer and myself went onto the field and I threw the ball, which barely made it to the catcher. The catcher ran up to me, handed me the ball, threw off his mask and got down on one knee. Needless to say, it was my boyfriend kneeling in front of me! He had the microphone in his hand and said "Heather, I love you very much. Will you marry me?" He pulled out the ring from behind him and placed it on my finger. I started crying and, for the moment, didn't care that there were four thousand people in the stands—it was just him and me. I said yes, and as we were walking off the field, he told me that all of my family and friends were there. It was the greatest moment in my life. —*Heather Cochrane & Dan Harper*

My Knight on Horseback

My boyfriend, Keith, and I live in Minnesota and were planning a long weekend in Las Vegas, where we would meet up with my parents. Knowing my parents wouldn't be there until late Friday night, we decided to take advantage of the time alone and go out to a nice dinner. He wouldn't tell me where we were going, except that I had to dress up really fancy. We arrived at a little Italian restaurant that overlooks the Las Vegas Strip, and the hostess led us to a table with a dozen of the most beautiful red roses I've ever seen on the table. When the hostess asked us if we'd like something to drink, Keith mentioned they should have something ready for us, and she brought out a bottle of my favorite wine that he had shipped up from southern California (which they would only do by the case).

After dinner, he said he had to take care of the bill, and as I sat waiting for him, looking at the sunset over the Strip, I saw him riding up the driveway on a white horse. Everyone in the restaurant knew what was going on except me, and the manager had to tell me to go outside, I was in so much shock.

When I got outside, he got off the horse, got down on one knee, and proceeded to ask me if I loved him,

114

would I love him forever, would I spend my life with him, would I be the mother to his children, and, finally, would I marry him. After all of that, I couldn't say anything, and all I did was nod my head as hard as I could while everyone from the restaurant was outside and witnessed it.

To top it off, my parents knew he was proposing, but only knew it was an Italian restaurant and there would be a horse. They got to Vegas early, and drove around for two hours until they found a restaurant with a horse trailer. They pulled up two minutes before Keith got on the horse and witnessed the entire thing. —*Jennifer Yannuzzi & Keith Kluzak*

The Romantic Rock Climber

This past summer I had the opportunity to travel and study in Brazil. Unfortunately, I had to leave my boyfriend of four years—we had been dating since our sophomore year in high school. After I arrived, I became very lonely and homesick. He would call me every night, but it just wasn't enough.

Then, while I was taking a walk on the most beautiful beach in Brazil, he called me on my cell phone. This beach was most famous for the romantic scenes and soaps that were filmed there. It was like the paradise that we see so much on TV. The beach has crystal clear water and large rock formations that couples like to climb on. I told him that I was on my way to the most famous rock formation and couldn't talk to him while I was climbing the rock, but that I would call him when I reached the top. When I reached the top, I called him, and he casually asked me if there was anything that people had left at the top. I told him that I saw a basket. We started to discuss whether I should open it and look inside. We decided that I should, and when I opened it, there was a ring box inside. I was amazed! I opened the box and, lo and behold, there was a beautiful diamond ring in it! I was so excited, and he was too.

Then my boyfriend appeared from over the other side of the rock with a cell phone in his hand, a grin on his face, and said, "Will you marry me?" I was so excited and surprised that I thought I might fall off the rock! But, even if I did, I knew that my honey would race to my rescue. He gave me a great big kiss and hug. We plan to marry in Brazil, at the same rock, in a year. —*Peggy Chen & David Yam*

The Invitation

It was the day before the one-year anniversary of our first date. After my car broke down on the way to work, an ugly way to start the day, Scott rescued me and promised the day would get better. When I got to my office, there was a small card sitting on my chair. I opened it and found a single rose petal, an invitation to dinner, and a quote glued to the blank inside: "Today is the after in happily ever after." The invitation read, "You are cordially invited to celebrate the one-year courtship of Mr. Scott Paul Hilsen and Ms. Laura Dale Maxwell at the Old Vinings Inn." Instantly my day began to brighten, but I was a bit confused as to why we would have a celebration dinner a day early.

Throughout the workday, little cards mysteriously appeared in the office mail, in my purse, and on my desk. Each contained a single rose petal and a romantic quote. With each one I opened, I swooned a little more in anticipation of the events to come. You might think I had a clue, but I didn't have the foggiest idea. Scott is a purebred romantic and has always made every occasion a full-blown event well beyond my wildest dreams or expectations. This was just the next one—or so I thought.

After work we stopped at a local bar for a relaxing drink with a friend before we moved on to our dinner engagement (no pun intended!). When we arrived at the quaint restaurant, he led me inside as he followed behind. I excused myself for a brief moment and returned to the hostess, who led me to our table and told me Scott would be right back. Scott sat down moments later and we made our wine selections. Once the wine was served, Scott interrupted me from the scrumptious menu to give me the last card of the day, only this one had a large ornate bow. I opened it to find another rose petal and a poem glued where the quotes had been before. Scott asked me to read it aloud.

I read the first stanza, which was filled with the most romantic sentiments I had ever read. I read the second stanza and realized he had written this poem himself, making reference to a star I renamed "Hilsen's Wish" for his birthday. When I began to read the last stanza, I realized this was more than just "Happy Anniversary." A chill ran through my bones and tears welled in my eyes as I quietly choked out the last few words he had written. But this stanza was different. It was missing the fourth line and the third ended with the word "destiny." In a moment, I looked up and found Scott next to me on one knee. Scott took my hand and held up a small glass box and said, "You are all my hopes and dreams. Will you marry me?"

I was completely overwhelmed. I said nothing. Scott, still awaiting my answer, opened the box and took out a beautiful diamond ring, which had been resting in the center of the remaining rose petals inside the glass box. Still I said nothing, completely beside myself in surprise and joy. As he placed the ring on my finger, I managed to answer through my tears, "I would love to marry you." Tears ran down my cheeks as I leaned down to kiss him for what seemed like forever.

When finally we broke apart and he sat back in his chair, I couldn't help but notice the couple next to us watching. Like a giddy schoolgirl I looked over and said, "Isn't this wonderful?" Scott and I cried and giggled and cried some more. For that moment, we were undoubtedly the happiest couple on Earth. We finally ordered but could barely touch our dinners for the excitement of the moment. I later found out that Scott arranged weeks before exactly where we would sit. He also arranged to have my favorite foods on the menu that week. (No wonder it was so hard to choose!)

We held hands over dinner and I rattled off rapid-fire questions like, "Who knew? When? Did you tell Mom?" while he struggled to tell me all he'd done in the last month. Then he stopped and gave me another gift, wrapped with a bow. I ripped the paper off to find the latest edition of the biggest wedding magazine he could find! Then, before I had the chance to thank him again, he pulled out one last present. It was the box the little note cards came in. The pattern on the outside was the same as the cards, a collage of Victorian romantic images, and, as if it were the title of a book, written across the top and spine were the words *A Romance*. I opened it and found seashell-shaped chocolates inside. I guessed the meaning right away— we were going to the beach for the weekend! To sweeten the pot, he told me he had already asked my supervisors for Friday off and we were leaving in the morning! The waitress offered dessert, but Scott politely told her dessert was at home.

When we got home, he opened the door and inside I saw my brothers, his parents, and our two best friends waiting to greet us with champagne toasts and dessert and coffee. The next morning we woke up, packed, and headed south for the beach. Shortly into the trip he brought my attention to the back windshield of the car. Written in white shoe polish were the words, "Just Engaged!" Yes, he thought of everything. We spent the weekend looking through magazines, setting dates, and enjoying the first days of the rest of our lives together.
—*Laura Maxwell & Scott Hilsen*

Written in Lights

My fiancé took my breath away with his proposal! I was a senior in college, finishing my business degree, and he was working nights at his job two hours away. I had just returned to school after the weekend, and when I walked into my Monday afternoon business law class, I was shocked to find two dozen red roses awaiting me! Tucked in the flowers was a card with instructions for me to go to Victoria's Secret at the mall, where I would find a package waiting for me. I could tell right away that the writing on the card was Tony's. That was the longest class I have ever had to sit through! Finally, class was over and I went to pick up my package. Wrapped up was something very feminine and with it was another card that instructed me to go back to my apartment, where I would find a favorite outfit that he had chosen for me to wear for an evening out. Laid out on my bed was a black skirt and jacket, along with all the accessories and another card. That card instructed me to meet him at the Freight House, one of the nicest dining places in town, at 7 P.M.

By this time, I thought I had a pretty good idea that something special was going to happen, so all afternoon I had been telling everyone I saw that I thought I was going to get engaged that night! I asked a girlfriend to drive me to the restaurant since I assumed that Tony would have his truck. He assumed that I would have my car—so he had another one of my friends drive him there and when we met, we both were without a vehicle! One of the girls drove him back to get his truck and she forewarned him that I was very suspicious and was expecting a proposal that night.

When Tony returned, we were seated at a candlelit table in the corner with a bottle of champagne. One of the first things he said was, "I heard a rumor that you think you are getting engaged tonight. I'm really sorry, but I just wanted to take you out before your finals next week." I tried not to look too shocked and at first I didn't believe him since this was not our typical Monday night date! All through dinner I was still expecting the proposal and kept looking for the ring, eyeing my food, the table, any place that he could have hidden it. Nothing happened! I was getting worried and I began feeling like I was wrong with my suspicions! We finally finished our meal and decided to drive around to look at Christmas lights and decorations. All I could think was what a fool I was going to look like the next day, having to tell everyone that no, I was not engaged. By the time we were finished and ready to head back to my apartment, my spirits were pretty low and it was hard to be in the Christmas mood! But Tony insisted that there was one more Christmas decoration I had to see, and it was right in front of my apartment!

On the lawn was the most beautiful Christmas decoration of all—a big sign made with four hundred red and white Christmas lights that said "Michella, will you marry me?" He parked the truck and got down on his knee and proposed! All of those lights weren't half as bright as the smile on my face! It was so exciting! My roommates were waiting for us—they were all watching out the window to see my proposal! After all the excitement and lots of pictures, we went inside to call my parents, and even though they tried to sound stunned, they knew what was going to happen and had been anxiously waiting for the phone to ring all evening! Tony had asked my dad for his permission to ask for my hand in marriage the day before and told them the details of his plans!

Tony and I are now busy planning for our wedding. I am so lucky to be marrying the sweetest and most caring man I know! Every Christmas I will be reminded of his special proposal, and there will never be another Christmas decoration that will take my breath away the way those red and white Christmas lights did that special night! —*Michella Rudolph & Tony Renchin*

Business or Pleasure?

I was on a business trip in Orlando last week. The four-year anniversary of our first date was Tuesday. I was a bit sad that I couldn't spend it with my man, but I figured we could celebrate when I returned. I called Dan at work from a pay phone, but he was out on an emergency sales call. I told the secretary I would call her with my hotel phone number once I checked in. I checked into my hotel and inside was a dozen long-stemmed roses and a bottle of wine. The card read, "Happy Anniversary, Honey, sorry I couldn't be there." I thought that was great, and had my friend take my picture so Dan could see the roses, since they might not make it back to New York with me. He called and I thanked him for the flowers. He had to run, but said he would call me later.

Dinner was spent with my good friend in the hotel restaurant. The waiter even brought me a cake with a candle because I told him it was my anniversary, but my man was not there. I took a picture of that too. Once back in the hotel room, I called Dan at home and left him a message saying that I missed him, and that I had an anniversary dinner without him and loved him. About fifteen minutes later, he called me (I figured he checked his messages). We spoke, and I told him my friend and I were heading to the bar for a few drinks. (They had this planned, but she didn't know about the ring!) I was sad and missed him, and told him I wished he were there. I hung up, then opened the door to go down to the bar. Outside my door was an envelope. Inside was a picture of my man and me, and a little voice recorder. He had recorded a message and sent me a picture to give me something to remember him on this day. He said he loved me very much and would see me soon. I thought it was so cute! My friend had to pull me out the door and put the recorder away.

We got to the bar and ordered drinks. Then the bartender brought over champagne from a secret admirer. There was a 1-900 number convention going on, so I thought we were getting picked up! I turned around after a minute of asking which man sent it, and there was my man! He looked so handsome, excited, and proud! He looked in my eyes, told me he loved me, pulled out a black box, opened it, took out the perfect ring, placed it on my finger, and asked if I would marry him. It was so beautiful and thoughtful. Needless to say, I couldn't move for a few minutes. He was only in town for twenty-four hours. It was the best business trip ever! The following Monday was my twenty-seventh birthday—talk about having a great week! —*Jill Cherveny & Daniel Keough*

On Broadway

My fiancé and I had been dating for approximately a year and a half. We had discussed getting married, but I never knew when he would pop the question. He told me that he had an early Christmas/Hanukkah (I am Catholic and he is Jewish) present—we were going to see *Grease* on Broadway. I was thrilled! I had been saying that I wanted to go for a long time.

The day before the show, my fiancé informed me that he had tickets for both my mother and my grandmother. I have to admit that I was a bit angry with him. You see, I work full-time (as does he); however, I go to school full-time, so this was going to be our one chance to actually have a night out, alone. Even though I wasn't thrilled about the idea of having my family along, we went anyway. My fiancé and I had front row seats, while my mom and my grandma were three rows behind us. Anyone who has ever been to *Grease* on Broadway in New York City knows that there is a show before the actual show. Once everyone sits down, an actor playing Vince Fontaine invites people onstage to enter a dance contest. After a great deal of persuasion, my fiancé convinced me to get up onstage in front of about one thousand people. We danced for about five minutes.

Vince Fontaine finally started narrowing it down. My fiancé and I and one kid were the only ones left. The kid won, but my fiancé and I had to stay onstage.

Then Vince Fontaine said that Mike (my fiancé) had called him that week, and he handed the microphone over to him. He got down on one knee, and told me that although we were two very different people, I was his best friend, and he wanted to marry me. I was shocked! I immediately started to cry. I don't even think I said yes, I just nodded my head. When we sat down he said that he had gotten my family tickets because he knew how important they were to me, and how it would be very meaningful to me for them to witness and share one of the happiest days of our lives!
—*Dana Febbi & Mike Boffard*

Alive and Loved

My proposal reminds me of how lucky I am to be not only loved, but also alive.

I lost the use of my right arm in a car accident and for the past five years I have never been able to get past the fact that I can no longer play the piano. I know that I'm fortunate because the accident could have been quite tragic, but as a classical pianist there is not much anyone can say to console me. My boyfriend has been very encouraging, but on the night that he proposed to me I was really not being receptive to his "don't worry, you are beautiful the way you are" story.

I was doing my exercises for my arm when he touched my right hand and asked me if I could feel anything. Of course, my response was no—the same answer that I had been giving him every other time he touched my right hand. Then he went into his pocket, grabbed my left hand, held out a ring and said, "Well, I'm sure that you can feel this hand, and I want to know if I can hold it for life. Will you marry me?"

I have never felt confident about myself until that breathtaking event. I feel that I have been extremely blessed. —*Sonja Baines & Michael Kuhleman*

The Safe Trooper

It was early August when I went to Georgia, where my boyfriend was completing an internship, to celebrate our three-year anniversary. We had been discussing getting married for about six months, and had decided that we wanted to get married the following summer. So, needless to say, I was expecting a little surprise! Our weekend began with a romantic picnic at Stone Mountain Park during the laser light show on Friday night. It was supposed to be a "group" event, but friends began bailing out, claiming "third-wheel syndrome." So the wheels in my brain began turning that afternoon, thinking tonight was the night. He came home from work with a dozen beautiful red roses and a big kiss. He then told me that another couple had decided to go, so I knew tonight was not "the night" after all. But it turned out to be a lot of fun anyway.

On Saturday, he had planned a surprise excursion for our anniversary. I woke up anxious and was very observant of every move he made. Absolutely nothing was out of the ordinary! We got in the car and proceeded to drive north. We ended up at a state park. It was gorgeous! We hiked through the woods and up to the top of the falls, where we took in the beautiful scenery and the cool weather. It was very romantic, but still there was no proposal. Next, we ventured to an old gold-mining town. It was very quaint and romantic. We walked from store to store, laughing and talking, and he began to explain how difficult finding a ring was. He basically told me to be patient and that it wouldn't be long. We ate lunch out on the deck of one of the town square's finest restaurants, yet not a hint of the big question. So by this time we were tired and ready to head home. When we got home, we only had about an hour to shower and change for dinner. I was exhausted! I asked him if we could go eat later, but he explained that the restaurant already had about an hour and a half wait. So I hurried to get ready.

We got to the restaurant and I couldn't believe my eyes. It was located directly on the Chattahoochee River. It had gorgeous landscaping and an awesome view. We sat outside by the river and had a glass of wine while we waited to be seated. He went inside to use the restroom, and left his camera case on the table. I saw a lump on top of the case, and like a sneaky child at Christmas, I felt it to see if it could be a little jewelry box. It was just the film! I was so ashamed and couldn't believe myself! After only thirty minutes, we were seated in a circular booth facing the water. Our meal was delicious and not a crumb was left on either of our plates from appetizer to dessert. We had a great time throughout dinner and had a wonderful conversation. Dessert had come and gone, and it was time to leave. I was a little disappointed. I began to realize that I had gotten myself worked up for nothing.

It had begun to rain pretty hard, so we had to run to the car. We started home, and he said he wasn't sure if we were going the right way. He was driving really slowly and the rain was really coming down. I told him what a wonderful day it had been and that I was very impressed with all his planning. I told him that he had really outdone himself. He was focusing on where he was going and I was reveling in the memory of the day when I noticed blue flashing lights in the rearview mirror. I immediately began to panic. He looked so scared and we both were worried about the fact that he had some wine at dinner. I rummaged through my purse and found a mint. We pulled into a strip mall and waited for the officer to come to the window. I began imagining the worst. What would I do if he got arrested or something? I couldn't believe that this was happening on our perfect day.

The officer asked for his license and my boyfriend asked why we were stopped. The officer said that we were driving "awfully slow." Give me a break! He questioned what my boyfriend was doing in Georgia with a Florida tag and driver's license. My boyfriend explained that he was doing an internship and would be returning to school in the fall. The officer asked him if he realized that Georgia tags and license were required after living in the state for thirty days! My boyfriend replied, "No sir, I was not aware of that." The officer began shining his flashlight in the car and asked if he had any weapons on him. "No, sir!" my boyfriend said.

Then the officer asked him to step out of the car. He put him up against the wall spread-eagle and began frisking him. I rolled down my window, which was facing them now. I was feeling helpless and worried that something wasn't right. The officer began patting him down from head to toe. He reached my boyfriend's pocket and pulled out a little black box, opened it, and asked me, "Ma'am, do you know anything about this?" I looked at the ring and then at my boyfriend and he had the biggest grin on his face and I knew that this had all been set up.

I simply sat there in amazement and began to cry! My boyfriend got down on his knee and said, "Will you marry me?" I was sobbing at this point and could not even speak. My boyfriend gave me a big kiss and hug, I said yes, and the officer reached in and asked for a kiss! I gave him a big kiss on the cheek and he told us to have a happy life! —*Lara Hunt & Michael Smith*

Disney World...Finally

In September of last year my now fiancé, Jeff, was the best man in a wedding in Springfield, Illinois. We made our usual wedding appearance and had a terrific time at the reception. Jeff and I had discussed marriage a few times but he always made it seem that he was uninterested at this point and wanted to wait a while before becoming engaged. The night of the wedding we had decided to get a room at the hotel where the reception was being held so we wouldn't have to drive home that night.

The morning after the wedding, Jeff and I had to get up early to take his cousin, Tom, and Tom's girlfriend to catch a return flight to Arizona. I threw my hair in a ponytail, threw on a T-shirt and shorts, and we were off to meet Jeff's family at his parents' restaurant to begin the two-hour journey to St. Louis. Oddly enough, his parents decided at the last minute to join us on the trip to see Tom and another of Jeff's cousins, Julie, off. We loaded up six adults in the car and started off. We dropped Tom and his girlfriend off at the gate, said our good-byes, and then began driving to the gate from which Julie (whose parents were bringing her to the airport) was departing.

About this time, Jeff's mother, Sandy, had an emergency restroom run and begged me to go with her into the airport terminal so she wouldn't get lost in all the confusion. Thinking nothing of it, I went with Sandy to the restroom while Jeff and his father parked the car. Sandy and I waited patiently for the guys to come into the terminal. Eventually Jeff's dad appeared, but Jeff was nowhere to be seen. His father explained that Jeff missed the parking lot, was circling around again and was in line to park. Again I thought nothing of it, and was sitting in the waiting area of the terminal with Jeff's parents when Jeff finally came walking up to us and said, "Annette, we are leaving for Orlando right now!" I thought he must have had too many drinks at the wedding reception the evening before, but then he pulled out the tickets and said again, "We are leaving right now for Orlando!"

As I was being swept up the escalator and to the boarding area, Jeff's parents were jumping up and down giggling about how sly they were to get me there. At this point, I was completely in shock and had tears streaming down my face. His cousin, Julie, really did leave out of the next gate so his uncle, aunt, and cousin were able to witness my reaction to the terrific surprise. Bewildered, I asked, "What about work?"

Jeff replied, "I already talked to your boss and it is all taken care of!"

Still worried and confused, I exclaimed, "But I don't have any clothes!"

He replied, "Your friends packed for you and they are already on the plane!" Jeff had planned this for quite some time and had asked my boss for the time off months ago. He also had asked my best friends to pack our bags while we were at the reception and deliver them to his parents, who loaded them into the car before we arrived that morning. (It made for some interesting outfits on the trip!)

As we were going through security, I was conveniently stopped and my bag was searched. I learned later that Jeff knew the ring box would set off the metal detector and the search of my purse was to divert my attention while he claimed the ring box on the other side. I had no idea he was wearing my ring on his pinkie as we made our way through the airport! Instead of parking the car, he was actually checking bags and going through security. Looking back now, I remember that there was constant discussion of spontaneous trips on the way to the airport, but I never put it together at the time. I also learned later that all the guests at the wedding the night before knew what was going to happen the next day. I still can't believe someone didn't spill the news.

On the flight Jeff told me that he wanted to take me to Disney World because I had told him that I always felt left out because I never went when I was a child. We arrived in Orlando late that evening and I couldn't sleep at all. I was almost nauseous because of all the excitement! The next day we went to Disney World. That evening, after the Disney light parade, while standing in front of Cinderella's castle with fireworks going off in the background and surrounded by tourists, Jeff dropped to one knee and asked me to do him the honor of becoming his wife. He is the most wonderful man I have ever known. —*Annette Lingleo & JeffreyFulgenzi*

The Fashion Show

To fully understand this story, you would have to have seen the movie, *Titanic*. But, who hasn't, right? Well, think back to the part in the movie where Jack is at the front of the ship, holding Rose's arms out, like she is flying. My fiancée, Amy, is a model for a bridal shop, and they do shows throughout the year. The latest theme for the show was for my fiancée to come out in a beautiful gown, walk to the front of the stage, and wait. Next, a male model would walk out and come up behind her. He would take her arms out to her sides, like the scene from the movie, then turn her around and hug her, then they would both walk off the stage together. And, of course, while all this was going on, Celine Dion's song would be playing in the background. I know the owner of the bridal shop well, thanks to Amy, and they thought it would be a great surprise if I took the male model's place and shocked Amy at their last show of the season. I agreed, of course, but I had an even bigger surprise in mind. After surprising Amy by being onstage, I would then go one better by proposing to her onstage in front of the whole crowd! The owners of the bridal shop thought it was an awesome idea, so we put the plan into works.

I got an engagement ring, asked her parents for her hand (I'm still a little old-fashioned), and then told Amy I wouldn't be able to make it to the show because of a job fair at college. The women from the bridal shop got me a tux, a bouquet of flowers, and I got the DJ to play a song for me. I was a wreck the night of the show, and I even got a surprise—a local TV news station showed up to film my proposal! Everything went beautifully. I hid backstage until the very end of the show, then, on cue, I walked up behind Amy and put my arms around her. When I turned her around, her jaw almost hit the floor! We hugged and kissed, and I started crying. Then the DJ played my song, which is about a guy who wants to propose to his girlfriend, but Amy was so excited about me being there that she didn't even hear the words. The music stopped and I got down on my knee, onstage, in front of about four hundred people and a TV camera. I make a little speech and asked Amy to marry me and, thank God, she said yes.

What makes this story even sweeter is that Amy was my high school crush. We sat across from each other in art class my junior year (her senior year). She graduated and I didn't see her for six years, until I happened to run into her at a bar one night. We talked all night, agreed to see each other the next night, and the rest has been even better than a fairy tale! —*T. Zalewski*

The Perfect Moment

My boyfriend and I have been together for ten years. Due to careers and very different lifestyles, we were not considering marriage. We never even lived together. This past year, we were once again faced with continuing our relationship in separate cities. But this time I couldn't adjust. I love James and I wanted to spend every moment with him. I knew James felt the same way. I even overheard a message on the machine from a jeweler. I eagerly waited for James to pop the question. Days turned into weeks, which turned into months, and he said nothing. I was devastated.

I decided that after the Christmas holidays I would confront him and tell him that I wanted to get married or it was over. Fortunately, it never came to that. James's birthday is in December and his brother suggested we throw him a surprise party. I thought it was a wonderful idea. I contacted his friends, who happened to be visiting that weekend anyway. Even my parents said they had business in a nearby town. People came from five different cities and I wasn't suspicious at all. My sister-in-law and I prepared a buffet. Our friends volunteered their house. James was unusually patient as I tried to stall for time by taking four hours to get ready.

The plan was to get James to our friends' house by telling him he had some friends over watching a fight. I was too pleased with myself to notice how quiet James was. He even acted surprised when we went inside and everyone yelled "Surprise!" About ten minutes later, James decided to open his gifts. I thought it was odd that he wanted to open them so soon, but it was his birthday. James opened his gifts as I chatted with my mom. All of a sudden, everyone got very quiet as James opened a foil-covered box. Then, he got down on his knee and asked me if I knew why everyone was there. I flippantly answered no. He asked two more times and I said no. Then, he leaned towards me and whispered in my ear "Everyone is here to watch me ask you to be my wife." He pulled a gorgeous diamond ring, which I learned later he designed and had made for me, out of the gift box. I was so surprised and happy that all I could do was nod my head yes. James had wanted to propose to me for months, but he wanted to propose at the perfect moment—so he created it.

Stars & Stripes Forever

The Monday before the Fourth of July, I got an invitation from my boyfriend to a special Fourth of July celebration. But, he said that I wasn't allowed to tell anyone about the invitation and that I should meet him outside my house at 5:30 A.M. on the fourth. At 5:30 A.M. on July 4, my boyfriend and his parents were waiting outside my house in their car. As we were driving, I noticed we were rather close to the airport and became a little suspicious. I asked him where we were going and he said, "We're flying to Charlotte." Since we live in Raleigh, and Charlotte is only two and a half hours away by car, I became even more suspicious. His parents dropped us off at the airport and when we got to our terminal, I discovered that Charlotte was our connecting flight to New York! I was completely floored.

We were in New York City by about 10:30 A.M. As it turned out, he had been researching this trip for several weeks on the Internet and knew exactly where to go and how much everything was going to cost. We took the subway to 77th and Lexington and walked to Central Park. We walked around for a little while, and eventually we came to the lake in the middle of the park. We rented a rowboat and he proposed to me under a little grove of trees in the middle of the lake. He got on his knee and everything. It was very romantic. After that, we spent the rest of the day sightseeing. We had lunch in Times Square, went to the top of the Empire State Building, and went to the Metropolitan Opera. That night we flew back to Raleigh, where both of our families met us at the airport.

Time Out for Love

For the 1997–98 NBA season, I was a dancer for the Houston Rockets basketball team. One night my mother and fiancé were coming to a game to watch me perform, but I had no idea that my fiancé and the other dancers had planned a surprise proposal for me that night. It just so happened that it was the first round of the playoffs and the game would be televised, not to mention that it was sold out.

During the game, the dancers were supposed to go out during a time out and perform with the mascot. He was going to dunk the basketball over us while we were blindfolded. They told me that I would be first in line since I was the shortest, which did not seem odd to me. So I was blindfolded, thinking the other girls were also, while really my fiancé was on the court handing out roses to the other dancers. During this, the crowd was really quiet, which seemed odd. Next thing I knew I was being turned around. They took off the blindfold and a huge painted sign was in front of me that said, "Allison, I love you, will you marry me? Love, Jason." Then, Jason burst through the sign and got down on one knee and asked me to marry him over the loud speaker and in front of sixteen thousand fans and pay-per-view

TV! I said yes and all the girls gave me the roses—and it all happened in about two minutes. It was the best night of my life and I even have the whole thing on video! —*Allison Brown & Jason Smiga*

Forty Pounds of Bird Seed

My fiancé had been secretly planning this big night for a week. I still can't believe that I didn't have a clue about what was going to happen. No one dropped any hints and all of my friends knew what was going on.

We started off the night with a nice dinner at an Italian restaurant. On our way back from dinner, my fiancé was acting a little strange and asking me funny questions, but I really didn't think anything of it. When we got back to my room, there was a huge red heart on the message board on my door that had our names in it—Kenny & Christine. I didn't think much of it; I knew it was my friend's handwriting and I thought she had put it up there just to be sweet. But when I opened the door to my room, I knew something was going on.

There were red and white crepe paper streamers all along the ceiling and strung across my dresser. Red and white balloons were all over—on top of my bed and covering the floor. On my dresser was a circle of red and white scented candles on top of gold doilies, burning around a beautiful bouquet of flowers. My bed was turned down and there was a single red rose on my pillow. In the background Pachelbel's Canon in D was playing on the CD player.

I was in complete shock. I had no idea he was about to propose. All I kept thinking was that he was way too early for Valentine's Day. He had to practically drag me over to the window where the freshly fallen snow was illuminated from the windows in my dorm. Out on the snow there was a huge birdseed heart (I later learned forty pounds of bird seed were used!) with the words "Will you marry me?" written in red Kool-Aid. He then got down on one knee and asked me to marry him. Of course, I was really crying by this time, but I managed to tell him yes in between the tears. The door then came flying open and all of my best friends and most of the floor came pouring into the room cheering. My friends all had their cameras flashing.

Ken made our engagement absolutely amazing. I love looking at all of the pictures that were taken of my wonderful engagement. No one had ever done anything so special for me before. It was the greatest night of my life.
—*Christine Sanfilippo & Kenneth Fales*

Beautiful Blue Bottle

Marc is from South Carolina, and every year he and all of his extended family rent a beach house just south of Myrtle Beach. This year he invited me to go along with them since we had been dating for ten months and knew we were serious about our relationship.

One night, he and I wanted to spend some time alone away from the family, so we walked along the boulevard, and then began walking along the beach. When we reached a set of rocks, Marc began taking his flashlight and searching around the rocks. At this point I thought he was looking for crabs and began to get tired and ready to head back to the house, but then I heard him exclaim, "I found something!"

"What?"

"A bottle!"

"A beer bottle?"

"No, an antique bottle!"

I walked over and he had picked up a beautiful blue bottle out of the sand. He opened it up and on parchment paper was an incredible love note to me. After I finished it in tears, he got down on his knee and said, "Amy Krista, will you be the bride of my youth and all my days? Will you marry me? Will you be my wife?" I said yes and we began hugging, and then he said to me, "Look over there," and pointed. Looking down the beach, I saw the largest fireworks display I'd ever seen! His family had been waiting for him to flash the flashlight as their signal to start our engagement with a blast. It was absolutely breath-taking. —*Amy Barnett & Marc Corbett*

Movie Night

Brian and I have opposite schedules. I work late nights, while he works the traditional 9–5 job. Usually, I am pretty wired when I get home around midnight or so but Brian has just enough energy to say, "Hi, how was your night…I love you, good night." One late Friday night in February, I came home completely exhausted. All I kept thinking about on the drive home was a shower and my bed.

Upon arriving home, I was quite surprised to see the house lit up like a Christmas tree. I was not even two feet in the door when Brian was already by my side, full of energy. He told me he borrowed a great movie from his parents, *A Prelude to a Kiss*, and that we should watch it. I muttered in a tired voice that I must take a shower first. While I was beginning to relax, I was thinking to myself how strange it was that Brian didn't even enjoy watching movies, but he seemed really excited about this. At this point, I was incredibly tired, but he knows how much I love movies, so I just sucked it up and watched it for him.

In the movie, two characters fall in love and decide to get married. Their wedding scene is about thirty to forty minutes into the movie. They have a beautiful ocean view ceremony and as the officiary is about to pronounce them man and wife, it cut into Brian talking to the audience (which, of course, is me).

At first I thought he had ruined his parents' copy of the movie by playing with the camcorder, but then I finally realized what was going on. He said all this mushy stuff about how we've been best friends for ten years and have dated for two years and it's time to get married. I was overwhelmed—I couldn't believe this was happening to me! Then he bent down on one knee in front of me and asked me to marry him. We had talked about getting married before, and I used to tell him that I would know when he was going to ask me, but I definitely did not see this coming! —*Regan Pelger & Brian Losty*

At the Falls

My fiancé, Rob, had been acting strangely for a few weeks, and I had a feeling he was getting ready to pop the question. One day, I came home from work to find a note waiting for me. The note read: "Stacie, the first place you need to go starts with a *b* and rhymes with *fluffalo*." Now, being a relatively intelligent person, I quickly figured out he meant Buffalo, but never having been there and not knowing anyone or anything in the area, this left me slightly confused. The note continued: "Hint: pack your suitcase and drive to the airport. There's an electronic ticket waiting for you at the United Airlines gate. Your flight leaves at 5:15 P.M. I'll meet you at the airport in Buffalo." I looked at the clock and realized I had one hour and fifteen minutes to get there. I quickly threw an odd assortment of clothes into a suitcase while calling as many people as I could in fifteen minutes.

I made it to the airport in record time and landed in Buffalo, New York, at 7:30 P.M. I got off the plane and started looking for Rob. He arrived a little after I did. He had left my apartment shortly after I'd left for work and driven the ten hours up to Buffalo. (Someone had told him it would only be a six-hour drive, and he thought it would be nice to have his car. Needless to say, it took longer than he thought.) Now, for those of you as clueless as I was, Buffalo is only thirty minutes away from Niagara Falls. We drove to our hotel, had dinner, and went to bed, never ever talking about why we were there.

The next morning, we had breakfast and then Rob said, "Are you ready to go to the Falls?"

Was I ever! We drove over to the Canadian side, walked as close as we could to the edge, and Rob dropped to one knee. He had several sheets of poster board with him. The first one said that he had written everything on poster board because he was afraid I wouldn't hear him over the sound of the falls. The next sign said how much he loved me and that he felt he was a better person when he was with me. The last sign read, "Will you marry me?" This was perhaps the most beautiful moment of my life. The falls were in front of me, the love of my life on one knee, and of course, I was crying. Then I realized we had an audience. There were about thirty people, all strangers, behind me and watching everything. They applauded when they saw the last sign. I stood there, speechless for a while, and then some guy called out, "Say yes!"

I looked at Rob, he looked at me, rather frightened, and said, "Well?" Of course, I said yes! We kissed and by the time we were done, the crowd had dispersed.

After we walked away, another couple came over and asked if we'd had anyone taking pictures, and we said no. They took my address and offered to send me the ones they'd taken, as well as the negatives. They arrived the other day, along with a very nice note. As wonderful as the whole trip was, it's that much better, thanks to that couple and the pictures they sent us! —*Caroline Dean & Robert Cameron*

Larger Than Life

Well, of course, since I've seen the movie *Titanic* four times, I'm a huge fan and I can't wait to see it again. My fiancé, Brian, called me up and said he had special plans for the weekend. When I asked him what we were doing, he was very vague at first. Then he said we were going to see *Titanic*. I was so thrilled because I want to see it as many times as I can and I didn't think I could get him to go see it again.

I live in San Diego and Brian lives in Los Angeles, so I drove up to see him for the weekend. That Saturday morning, we woke up and got ready for our fun outing. Then, as we were getting in the car, he handed me a blindfold and asked me to put it on. I love surprises, so I complied and then we drove for about fifteen minutes. I had no idea where we were, but soon the car stopped. Brian opened the door for me and helped me out of the car. He spun me around and told me I could take the blindfold off. When I removed it and looked up, there before me was the biggest ship I had ever seen. I was so excited, I started jumping up and down and yelling, "It's the Titanic!"

Brian looked at me and said, "I never said we were going to see *Titanic* the movie!" We were at the Queen

Mary in Long Beach, which is where we spent the night. We got to see the Titanic exhibit onboard and a documentary. Then that night, Brian proposed to me under the stars on the bow of the ship, which had been cordoned off so no one else was there. It was titanically romantic! —*Erika Kozain & Brian Robinson*

Love is Kind of Crazy with a Spooky Little Girl Like You

My fiancé, Bob, and I met in the high school drama department. He was fourteen, while I was a more mature fifteen, so I only viewed him as a sweet, funny guy who was a good pal. My junior year of high school, we did a play in which Bob and I were cast as ill-fated lovers. Our first kiss was onstage in front of loads of people and Bob thought it was a great chance to let me know how much he looked forward to rehearsing that scene. The next year was my senior year and Bob and I became more than friends. We went to the Valentine's dance together and Bob told me that I looked like Miss America. I thought that was kind of goofy, but he was only sixteen years old and had a sad case of puppy love.

I graduated and we went our separate ways. We still saw each other on occasion and we dated a couple of times. He went on to become a journalist and I tried to finish my theater degree. I went through a bad relationship and Bob was always willing to listen and give advice, even though he was a thousand miles away. We would get together when he came home or I would go visit him in Savannah. Eventually, we both ended up in Savannah—Bob had a fun job at an entertainment newspaper and I gave tours on horse-drawn carriages.

On Halloween night, I was telling ghost stories on a carriage tour while another girl drove the team of horses. We parked the horses in front of Colonial Cemetery, the oldest cemetery in Georgia. I was relating one of my favorite Savannah ghost stories when a figure dressed in colonial clothing emerged from behind a tree carrying a candle. I laughed and said it must be the ghost of James Oglethorpe, when all of a sudden, the figure called my name. I realized it was Bob and became very confused. I asked him what the heck he was doing, but he simply took my hand and helped me down from the carriage. He got down on one knee and said, "Love is kind of crazy with a spooky little girl like you. Will you marry me?" I said yes, even though I was shaking and crying. The tourists were all clapping and friends of mine who were hiding behind the trees told me that they had known about it all day. I had no idea. I had even tried to get out of working that night!

It was a beautiful night in the gorgeous historic district with the Spanish moss swaying in the trees, the horses clip-clopping along, and Bob giving me a lovely ring and asking me to be his wife. It was very dramatic, which fits our personalities. I am sure our lives will hold even more drama and comedy to come. —*Lorretta Gaskins*

Picnic in the Park

Anthony and I had been talking about getting married for a few months. We would both start talking about it with these two words—*one day*. He always surprises me with different and romantic things to do. So one beautiful Saturday in September, he suggested going on a picnic, which we've done many times. I brought some cheese and crackers and he said he'd bring the wine. We got to the park and he opened the trunk of his car and took out a beautiful picnic basket that had balloons that said "I love you" tied to it. I thought that was very sweet and I asked him why he did it. He said that he always loves to surprise me and tell me in little ways how much he loves me.

We found a spot to sit in the park behind a beautiful pine tree and he pulled out a nice bottle of wine and crystal glasses, as well as his cassette player, on which he had taped love songs. We sat there quietly for a moment, drinking our wine and just looking at each other. He then pulled out two papers from the basket. He told me that one day when he was waiting for me to come home from work, he decided to write a "history" of our life together until this point. In this letter, he wrote how we met, how he felt about me from the beginning, and how he fell in love with me. He said he would continue the letter every year. It brought tears to my eyes. Then, when he was done, he said, "I have a few more things to show you." He then pulled out a three-by-five-inch ceramic picture frame with a bride and groom's picture in it—with our faces! Then he pulled out a miniature bottle of champagne and two miniature glasses and said, "One day people will be toasting us." Then he got on his knee and pulled out a teddy bear with my engagement ring tied around its neck and started telling me how much I mean to him. Meanwhile, "Always and Forever" was playing on the cassette (which, of course, is now going to be our wedding song). He then asked me to marry him. I was crying and, of course, I said yes! To me, this was the most romantic proposal anyone could ever receive! —*Linda Gitlin*

The Wooden Bowl

Aaron and I first began dating when I was a junior in high school and he was a freshman in college. After four months, I decided that it was not working out, so we stopped dating. Almost a year later, I received a letter from him, and decided to give friendship between us a chance. Ever since the second "first" date, I have been falling in love with him more and more. His proposal to me was better than I could have ever imagined.

One weekend in January, Aaron came back from college to see me, as usual. He asked me to go out to eat with him Saturday night. I asked him how I should dress, and he told me to wear something nice. This was nothing out of the ordinary, so I didn't suspect anything. He was late picking me up, which is not his nature at all. (I later found out the reason he was late is because he went by my father's work to ask him for my hand in marriage.) He took me to his aunt's house. There was no one there, and the dining room was set elegantly for a romantic dinner. He prepared our dinner while I was there—steak, salad, bread, cheesecake, and red wine.

After a short conversation following dinner, he went into the kitchen and brought out a wooden bowl and a pitcher filled with water. He took off my shoes, poured the warm water into the bowl, and proceeded to wash my feet. While he was doing this, he told me the story in John about how Jesus washed the disciples' feet as an act of servanthood. Then he told me that he wanted to serve me for the rest of my life. I started to tear up. After he dried off my feet, he reached into his pocket and pulled out a white box. Of course, by now I knew what was happening. I immediately burst into tears, because the moment I had been waiting for had finally arrived! He put the ring on my finger, and I finally was able to say yes. In the wooden bowl, he had written a message with a wood burner: our names, the date of the proposal, John 13 and Mark 10. This was a moment truly blessed by God, as will be our wedding day. —*Natalie Lentz & Aaron Wall*

I Know a Place

It was one of those ridiculously hot July evenings in Houston about five years ago. At 8:00 P.M., the temperature approached ninety-four degrees, having been around one hundred degrees for most of the day. I suggested that Tamara be ready at 9:00 A.M. on Saturday for a "date." At the appointed time, and with "his and her" bags prepacked (do not attempt to try this at home) and secreted in the trunk, we headed not toward the brown muddy waters of Galveston to cool off, but north, toward the airport. Sitting two gates away but within hearing distance of the final boarding call, we hurried last minute onto the runway, Tamara still without a clue as to destination. We landed in El Paso, admittedly not the first place you think of for a romantic getaway and which was also enjoying a heat wave. I rented a car and we drove to Ruidoso, New Mexico, in time for dinner at the Inn of the Mountain Gods, run by the Apache Indian tribe. Sensing that this was "the dinner," Tamara carefully, and nervously, checked her champagne glass, the entrée, the dessert, the flowers, etc., for a ring. I think she also surveyed the area around our table to see if I had enough room to kneel (she denies this).

The next morning, we drove to the Sierra Blanca Mountains where a seventy-six-year-old guide and his thirty-six-year-old Indian wife had saddled four horses, one of them with a bottle of champagne in a saddlebag. The "odd couple" rode (and bickered) halfway up the mountain with us, where we stopped to fly fish (part of the package), and then sent us on our way to the top. The weather became drizzly and damp as we made our way up the peak, with the champagne sloshing in the saddlebag. When we broke out of the tree line, we encountered one of the most beautiful mountain horizons south of the Colorado Rockies. The skies had even cleared. There, on a rocky ledge overlooking some of God's finest work, I got down on one knee and asked Tamara if she wouldn't mind spending the rest of her life with me. Tears welled up in her eyes. She says I cried too (I deny this). She said yes and her hand shook as I placed the ring on her finger. Although the champagne spewed everywhere, it added a very nice touch on that cool afternoon in the New Mexico mountains. So, when Houston heats up in the summer, I know a place...

Appendix:
"Will You Marry Me?"

Those four little words form what may well be the most important question you'll ever ask. The rest of your life flows from that question. It joins two families and begins a new family, and determines everything from what you'll eat for dinner, to where you'll spend your holidays, to what your children will be like.

In other words, this question and the way it is asked is a BIG DEAL—too big to treat casually. You don't want to just pull out the ring box while you're watching TV and say, "Oh, yeah, I thought you might like to, uh, y'know...would you?"

Make it a moment you'll both remember forever!

She will remember it, every tiny detail of it—the weather, what she was wearing, what you were wearing, the time, the place, everything. She'll remember whom she told first and what they said, how her parents reacted, and how your parents reacted—everything! So take the time and make the effort to plan it, and make the details come out right. Why spend a lot of time and money getting the perfect diamond only to have the Big Moment turn out to be a flop? The diamond is just one part of the Perfect Proposal. It takes thought, planning, loving attention to detail, and occasionally teamwork to create the kind of fireworks that will leave a lasting glow on your lives together.

Planning the Perfect Proposal: A Worksheet

Attire

Will you wear a tux? Maybe a gorilla suit to say that you're not monkeying around? Make a statement with your wardrobe.

Budget

Do you rent a plane or a limo? Take her to the most romantic restaurant? Feed her champagne and caviar? Determine what you can afford to spend on a once-in-a-lifetime occasion.

Location

Very important! The observation deck of the tallest building in town? A hilltop under the stars? On the deck of a sailboat? On a moonlit beach? Don't forget, it can be a "combo"—first a restaurant, then the beach, for example.

Day & Time

Pick a day that's special to you, such as the anniversary of your first date. Or evening, when a full moon rises over the lake.

Food

Taking her to the first restaurant you went to together can be fun. Cooking her a meal is a sure winner!

Flowers

Absolutely! Whether it's great bouquets of flowers or a single red rose, flowers are a must for romantic moments.

Candy

Find out what her favorite is, and present it as a treasure, wrapped in gold paper and tied with a bow, even if it's a Snickers bar.

Accessories

Take along a cellular phone so she can call her mother or her sister. She'll be bursting to tell everyone! If you can, set up a video camera to record the moment.

Scrapbook

Write down all the details of the moment—details that you (and your children) will savor in years to come. Include newspaper headlines from the day you got engaged.

Engagement Facts

• Approximately 2,400,000 couples wed in the U.S. each year.
• One-third of all couples become engaged during the last quarter of the year, October through December.
• The average age of a man getting engaged is 26.5 years; the woman's average engagement age is 24.4.
• The average price of a diamond engagement ring is $1,597. If the engagement ring is purchased as part of a bridal set, the average price is $880.

Five Proposal Styles

Over the years, I've come across five basic styles of proposals. Which best describes your situation?

The Total Surprise

She doesn't know it's coming —not a clue, not a hint. You've never even discussed it. This is gutsy! It reminds me of the school dances of my youth, where all the girls were on one side of the gym and all the boys stood on the other. You'd finally get up the nerve to make that long walk across the floor to ask a girl to dance. If she said no, and they often did, the walk back across the floor was very, very long.

I figure fewer than 10 percent of all proposals are in this category. It's like doing a high-wire act without a net. Most guys drop hints first, or get hints from her that indicate which way the wind is blowing. But there are the big risk-takers, the guys who live on the edge, who just go out and buy the ring and make the dinner reservations and GO FOR IT! Hurrah for them, but I have to tell you I don't recommend popping the question "cold."

Great Proposal #1

"Beach Party"

On a warm September evening, Peter takes Susan to dinner at their favorite restaurant, the dining room of an elegant inn on the coast of Maine. The maitre d' tells them their table will be ready in a half hour, and suggests a stroll on the beach while they wait. As they amble down the short path from the inn to the beach in the soft last light of the day, they hear violins playing "their song." On the beach they find a string quartet in tuxedos playing to a table, candlelit and elegantly set for two, with a vase of red roses in the center and a bottle of champagne chilling in a silver ice bucket. When they reach the table, Susan gasps as she reads the place cards: "Susan" and "Peter." They sit, Susan's amazement growing by the minute. Peter pours champagne and offers a toast to their love, then pulls a particular red rose from the vase and presents it to her. She inhales the fragrance of the rose, then, as she discovers the beautiful diamond ring tied to the stem of the rose with a white silk ribbon, she hears the magic words: "Will you marry me?"

She Knows

You've talked about getting married, you know you both want to get married and spend your lives together, you've talked about having kids, you've pledged your undying love. The only thing she doesn't know is when it's coming.

Men, the time between when she knows you'll give her a ring and the moment when you actually give it to her can be one of the greatest times of your life. Have some fun! Keep her guessing, plan the moment well, and when she least expects it, spring your wonderful surprise.

Great Proposal #2

"Breakast at Tiffany's"

One Saturday morning, Sam picks up his girl-friend Marie. They have planned to run errands, but instead Sam takes her to a jewelry store where the sales manager escorts them to a private room. There, Marie finds a table set with candles, flowers, and champagne—plus a selection of six diamond engagement rings, all in her size, arranged on a fine china plate. Sam drops to one knee, and proposes. Marie happily accepts, and Sam pulls out a chair for her, pours a glass of champagne, and tells her to choose her engagement ring—any one of the beautiful sparklers on the plate before her.

Let's Elope!

"Will you marry me? Right now? Tonight?"

Wow! This one makes no sense to me unless:

- ❧ The Early Pregnancy Test came up positive.
- ❧ *America's Most Wanted* is profiling you tonight.
- ❧ It's her fifth marriage, your seventh.
- ❧ You don't want to give her a chance to change her mind.
- ❧ Desert Storm II has broken out and you love her her so much you can't wait.

It's Now or Never

Way to go—you've waited so long she's resorting to threats: "We're getting married or I'll find someone who'll appreciate me!" Fish or cut bait, guy. If you love her, get off the fence and show her you can't live without her. If it's come to the threatening stage, you have to be extra, extra romantic to make up for her long wait. Use my proposal planning worksheet and make it a good one!

Great Proposal #3

"Birthday Wish"

Nicole raced home from work early to get ready for a romantic evening on the town with her boyfriend, Devin. It was her birthday! He had told her to "dress up" because he was taking her to a fancy restaurant. At the appointed hour, the doorbell rang, and in stepped Devin in a snazzy tux, bearing roses and an armload of gifts. He produced a bottle of champagne and suggested they sit on the couch, drink a toast to her birthday, and she could open her birthday gifts.

The first gift was a new dress that Devin had picked out for her. She loved it! She opened the next present—a sexy negligée. Then came a new best-selling novel (she's a voracious reader). Finally,

Devin handed her a small, elegantly wrapped box. Nicole's eyebrows raised a millimeter or two—it was obviously a jewelry box, and she loves jewelry. She carefully removed the wrapping to discover the familiar blue box that is Tiffany's hallmark, and her heart beat just a tiny bit faster. Opening the box, she saw winking up at her a sterling silver key ring with a sterling heart pendant, and on the heart was engraved—her birthdate. How romantic! But there was a much bigger surprise in store. When she took the key ring from its little box she turned it over and looked at the other side of the heart. Engraved on that side were the words *Marry me!*

Ringless

You and your True Love are in each other's arms, caught up in a rising tide of passion. The dialogue goes like this:

"Honey, I love you!"

"I love you, too, sweetheart."

(Kiss kiss smooch kiss)

"I can't live without you!"

"Oh, baby, you're the only one I'll ever love!"

(Smooch kiss smooch kiss)

"I want all our days to be like this."

"Oh, sweetie, I do too!"

"Will you marry me?"

"Yes! Oh, yes, yes, yes!"

But does Romeo have a ring in his pocket? Nooooooo. So where do we go from here?

Don't think this lets you out of getting her a ring! Get that thought out of your head right now!

A lot of ringless proposals lead to a couple shopping together for the ring. Or, you could revert to the "She Knows" proposal and keep her guessing. Either way, the ringless proposal shouldn't be ringless for long.

Great Proposal #4

"The Twelve Days of Love"

This is a romantic variation on the Twelve Days of Christmas, in reverse. Twelve days before he planned to propose to Ellen, Tim began sending her gifts. Each day, a limo would arrive, and a uniformed butler would step out bearing an anonymous gift. First, twelve red roses. Then came eleven love poems, ten pieces of Godiva chocolate, nine porcelain boxes, eight champagne flutes, seven cuddly teddy bears, six silk scarves, five silver charms, four scented soaps, three bottles of perfume, two pearl earrings—and finally, on the twelfth day, Tim arrived in person, dressed as the butler, bearing one bottle of champagne, one Very Important Question, and one diamond ring.

Great Proposal #5

"On the Radio"

Dave called the evening DJ at the radio station he and Tina always listened to and enlisted his collaboration. As Dave and Tina were in the car, heading for dinner, the DJ began playing the pre-recorded interview he'd done with Dave. On the tape, Dave is telling the DJ about his wonderful girlfriend—the story of how they met and everything about her. Tina gradually realizes that this story sounds familiar. Then she realizes it's Dave's voice she's hearing on the radio! Dave continues driving, grinning from ear to ear as Tina listens in astonishment. Finally, over the radio, Dave's voice says, "Tina, open the glove compartment." She does, and finds a ring box. "Open it," Dave's voice commands. Inside is a beautiful diamond ring. Finally, Dave's voice comes over the radio asking, "Tina, will you marry me?"

Great Proposal #6

"No Time for a Practical Joke"

I'm known as the "Jokester" to all my family and friends, which is why, when it came time to propose, I mixed romance with a practical joke.

Anyway, here's my story. I'm not proud of what I did, and I'm lucky to have the sweetest, most tolerant, loving, and understanding woman by my side. (Except that day when she jumped overboard into the cold, murky water of the Atlantic, but I'm getting ahead of myself.)

Katie and I have been buddies ever since she moved next door to me in the second grade. Through grade school, high school, and college, we've always been a team. So just before her thirtieth birthday, I decided to pop the question and join that special fraternity, "I'ma Hitched Too." So I went out and got the biggest and best ring I couldn't afford and started to plan the proposal.

You see, my family has a beautiful yacht that we go sailing on, and I felt that would be the perfect place to propose and pull my practical joke. I figured I'd have all of her family and my family onboard, get her by the rail, get down on one knee, pull out the ring, and pop the question. Then, at that precise moment, her brother would walk up, say, "Let me see!" and I would knock her ring into the ocean. Well, not really her ring, but a fake that I'd have switched for the real one. I figured once she started to panic, I'd pull out the real McCoy, and everyone would laugh and cry. Well...it didn't go according to plan.

It was a beautiful day for sailing—seventy-two degrees, sunny, not a cloud in the sky. I told Katie that I had lined up both our families to spend a little time together. Everyone was to meet at the docks at noon. By 1:30, we had finished lunch, and I was ready for plan "switcheroo." Alex, my soon-to-be brother-in-law, was ready, so I led Katie to the rail to see the view.

"Katie, I've known you all my life," I began, as I got down on one knee and took her hand. "And you know that you are the most important person in the world to me." Her hand began to tremble, and her eyes started to water. "I love you with all my heart, and you would make me the luckiest man if you would be my wife!" At that moment, I removed "The Fako" from my pocket (I had tagged the boxes too, as not to make a mistake) and showed her the ring.

"Let me see! Let me see!" said her brother as, on cue, he knocked the ring overboard. What happened next, I could not have planned. Little five-foot, two-inch, 105-pound Katie dove into the water to recover her ring! We all stood in shock for a moment before it hit us that she had just jumped into the ocean. I jumped in after her, my father jumped in after me, and her father jumped in for safe measure.

When we were all pulled safely aboard, Katie was in tears, "My ring! My beautiful ring is gone." I reached into my pocket and produced the real thing and told her what I had done. Instead of the punch in the face that I deserved, she cried even more, threw her arms around me, and said, "I love you!"

I am the luckiest man in the world!

Great Proposal #7

"Wasn't Going to Wait Forever"

My name is Fran. Ashton and I have been dating for nine years. He says he's comfortable with our relationship. Well, I'm not! Every third Wednesday of the month, Ashton plays in a poker game. I contacted his buddies and told them what I was up to. They agreed emphatically.

My plan was to get my girlfriend Sally, who works for the costume department at Universal, to make me up like a man so I could play in the poker game. Then, during the game, I would make my move. Fortunately, my dad taught me how to play poker, so I wouldn't be a novice at the game.

"Ashton, this is Frank. He's going to be playing with us," said Dave, the game leader. I was petrified under my baseball cap, fake beard, and nose that he would find me out, but he was none the wiser.

After about an hour of playing, Dave, a pretty good card manipulator, dealt Ashton and me two great hands. Of course, I had the better hand. (He had four kings, I had four aces!) The betting went wild. Everyone else folded, and it was just he and I, with over one thousand dollars in the pot.

"I hate to do this to ya, fella, being that you're new to the game, but I've got four kings," Ashton said and reached for the money.

"Not so fast," I said in a deep voice. "Where I come from, four aces beat four kings." I then laid down my hand. All the blood left his face as he fell back in the chair.

"But," I said, "I'll tell you what. You can keep the money if you do just one thing."

"Oh, yeah," he sat up. "What's that?"

I began to remove my disguise. "If you marry me and make me the happiest woman in the world."

"Oh my God! Fran! It's you!"

I repeated, "Will you marry me?"

"Oh honey, of course I'll marry you," he said as he hugged and kissed me. "But what about all of this money?"

"You're going to need it to help you with my new ring that we are going shopping for tomorrow!" I informed him.

We both laughed and cried. I really am the luckiest woman in the world.

About the Author

Fred Cuellar, the founder and president of Diamond Cutters International, is one of the world's top diamond experts. Diamond Cutters International (DCI) is one of America's few diamond houses open to the public by appointment only. He is an importer and creative designer of jewelry. His clients include the Saudi Royal Family and hundreds of professional athletes. Mr. Cuellar is accredited in diamonds and colored stones by the Gemological Institute of America and is ranked as one of the top diamond experts in America by *National Jeweler*. He is also the author of the No. 1 selling book on diamonds in the country, *How to Buy a Diamond*.

Other Books By the Author

Diamonds for Profit

Diamonds for Profit will benefit any reader who wants to sell (or buy and sell) diamonds or colored-stone jewelry—from the one-time seller to the entrepreneur. With *Diamonds for Profit* as your guide, you can make money buying and selling diamonds! It will show you how to determine the immediate cash liquidity value of your jewelry so you don't get talked into buying them for less. Also learn how to treasure-hunt for diamonds and jewelry in the classified ads, going-out-of-business sales, and national and local estate auctions in your spare time—and make money at it!

The price is $23.95.

Fredisms

Fredisms is the culmination of a personal life experience which you will be intrigued to discover as you read the Fredism on each page of this uniquely formatted book. Mr. Cuellar touches upon subjects of interest to us all, such as attitudes, health, humor, relationships, God, philosophy, and many others, in a way which will endear the book to a wide variety of readers. It will make a great gift for almost anyone and is easy to read. In fact, you will probably find yourself repeating your most favored Fredism to family and friends before long!

The price is $14.50.

How to Buy a Diamond, 3rd Edition

Buying a diamond can be one of the most important and intimidating purchases you ever make. Whether you're getting engaged or buying for an anniversary, investment or "just because," *How to Buy a Diamond* will take the pressure and uncertainty out of getting the best diamond for your money.

Newly revised and completely updated, *How to Buy a Diamond* is a simple-to-use insider's guide to buying the right diamond at the right price. This valuable resource provides the information you need to understand the terms of the industry, choose a jeweler and get a stone that won't leave you feeling cheated.

Important sections include:
- Matching your funds with the perfect diamond
- Wholesalers' secret pricing guides (charts the public never gets to see!)